Choosing to Prosper

Triumphing over Adversity, Breaking out of Comfort Zones, Achieving Your Life and Money Dreams

Bola Sokunbi

WILEY

Published by John Wiley & Sons, Inc., Hoboken, New Jersey.
Published simultaneously in Canada.

For general information on our other products and services or for technical support, please contact our Customer Care Department within the United States at (800) 762-2974, outside the United States at (317) 572-3993 or fax (317) 572-4002.

Wiley also publishes its books in a variety of electronic formats. Some content that appears in print may not be available in electronic formats. For more information about Wiley products, visit our website at www.wiley.com.

Library of Congress Cataloging-in-Publication Data is Available:

ISBN 9781119827368 (Hardback)
ISBN 9781119827382 (ePDF)
ISBN 9781119827375 (ePub)

Cover Design: Joyce Teo
Cover Image: © Angelito Jusay

SKY10034673_071322

This book is dedicated to the women in my family who came before me and set the stage for who I am and what I have accomplished today. To my grandmothers, my aunties, and my incredible mother. Thank you. I also dedicate this book to every woman choosing to prosper, and I hope my story and my journey so far serves as inspiration.

Contents

About the Author

Bola Sokunbi is a certified financial education instructor (CFEI), investor, finance expert, speaker, podcaster, influencer, and the founder and CEO of Clever Girl Finance, a personal finance platform created to empower women to achieve real wealth and live life on their own terms.

She started Clever Girl Finance in 2015 to provide women with the tools and resources she wished she had when she began her financial journey.

She is also the author of the bestselling books *Clever Girl Finance: Ditch Debt, Save Money, and Build Real Wealth; Clever Girl Finance: Learn How Investing Works, Grow Your Money;* and *Clever Girl Finance: The Side Hustle Guide: Build a Successful Side Hustle and Increase Your Income.*

Today, she lives with her husband and twins in New Jersey.

Acknowledgments

Writing a book is hard, and this one was particularly challenging because, unlike my three previous books, this is based on my personal story. Thank you to my parents for fact checking, sharing their own stories with me, and raising me to be who I am today, to my husband for encouraging me throughout this entire business building journey, to my twins who always tried to keep very quiet whenever Mommy was working on her book, and to my dearest and closest sister-friends, who have never stopped supporting and cheering me on. From the texts and the phones calls encouraging me to keep going, to just always being there for me. I love and appreciate you.

To my advisors and big sisters, Maureen, Roshi, and Monique. Thank you, Maureen, for helping me lay out the initial outline for this book after I called you out of the blue to say I was stuck. Thank you, Roshi, for brainstorming book names with me over email, text message, and on the phone. And thank you, Monique, for reminding me about why I needed to write this book to share my voice. You have been with me on this journey, building Clever Girl Finance, and I appreciate you.

To my other amazing advisors, Dan, Jonathan, and Brent. Thank you for your advice, for constant words of encouragement, and for supporting this female-owned and female-focused business!

A massive thank-you to the Clever Girl Finance team for holding down the fort while I spent months focused on writing. Thank you, Esther, Yazmir, Anita, Stacy, Carli, and Kat. And thank you to all our incredible writers and content creators. You make Clever Girl Finance work.

To my development editor, Cassidy Horton, thank you for your feedback and motivation and for helping to make this a book I'm proud of.

To my managing editor, Kevin Harreld, for pushing me to write this book now, and to the rest of the incredible Wiley team that has supported me on my journey as a now four-time author—thank you so much.

Introduction: You Have to Tell Your Story

Be empowered and bold and know you have a voice that no one can make you bury.

As a child, I thought I would grow up to be a doctor. It was a big dream of mine. I would line up my dolls in my pretend doll hospital and treat them for made-up ailments. I was a great doll doctor. But in real life, the sight of blood made me queasy and I quickly realized that career path was a no-go for me. I wasn't sure what else I wanted to do until one day in high school in Nigeria, my dad brought a Compaq desktop computer home for our family. It was a massive thing with a standalone central processing unit that hummed and purred, but it was new and exciting. After spending hours and hours on the computer each weekend, I taught myself how to use MS DOS (Yup, it was the mid-1990s!) from books my dad bought me. With my love for computers, I wound up deciding to study computer science and business with a certification in website development when I got to college. That decision was inspired by both my parents, who would always tell me, *"Bola, computers are the future, but if that doesn't work out, you can always fall back on business."*

My dad was a PhD-holding mathematician, econometrician, and later the head of the technology department at the government job where he worked. He was educated in Nigeria, Russia, and the United States. My mom, on the other hand, studied economics, had a master's degree in finance, and got her education in Nigeria, Austria, and the US. She worked in investment banking in Nigeria, building side hustles to earn extra income along the way.

At first glance, we were a pretty middle-class Nigerian family. But there's a whole backstory behind how my parents got to where they were as the first generation of middle class in my family. While I go deeper into my family and personal background story throughout the course of this book, I'll set the stage here.

My dad didn't start primary 1 (the first grade) until he was 13 years old. The reason? My paternal grandfather was not a fan of colonial education (inherited from the British Colonial rule in Nigeria). It also cost a lot of money, which he didn't have. So instead of school, my dad worked on his father's farm to help support his family. It was only after much convincing, and well over a decade later, that my grandfather allowed him to go to the closest school in the next town a few miles away while my grandmother supported paying his school fees with the little money she made as a small-goods trader. He made the journey to school every day on foot.

My mom, who was fortunate enough to start her schooling when she got to school age, met my dad and got married at 19 with only a high school diploma. She didn't start college until after she had her four children and was in her mid-thirties. She came upon the realization that she needed to be able to stand on her own two feet financially, and she saw education as a pathway to get there.

Both of my parents come from polygamous families and had parents that were not formally educated, making them both the first generation to go to grade school, high school, and college in their respective families. Poverty was also a familiar experience for them both growing up. And as soon as they graduated from high school and were able to earn any form of wages doing odd jobs here and there, they were obligated to support their younger siblings. Knowing about my parents' backgrounds and all the sacrifices they'd made to give me and my brothers a better life than they had growing up, I knew I had to do well. That was all they asked of me.

So, over the course of 11 years after graduating college, I worked as a test engineer, a technology consultant, and a business analyst. In most cases, I was the only woman on my team or in my department. I faced all kinds of prejudice, sexism, and racism. I was underestimated and opposed because of my gender. I struggled to find peers or mentors in my workplace that I could relate to as a woman of color. And many times, I struggled with the isolation of being the only one: the only black person, the youngest person, the only woman. And so, I retreated into my shell and just focused on the job I needed to do. I focused on doing it well, so that when I called my parents, I could tell them everything was great.

But despite my challenges, I loved the work I did. I felt a sense of exhilaration for every problem I investigated and solved and for every solution and strategy I presented that was implemented—even when others took credit for my work. And for a while, I was pretty content, keeping to myself at work, making good money, climbing my career ladder slowly but surely, and doing well.

However, as time passed, I became less and less content, and I felt something was missing. Sure, my parents were proud of me and I was making decent money. But I wanted to be more than just a number in a payroll file managed by a human resources department that could pull my file and fire me at any time if the company hit a bump in the road. I was tired of retreating and conforming at work. I was also going through my own personal life transitions. I had gotten married, moved cities, and become a mother to my beautiful twins. Time was flying by and life was happening, and I wanted to make sure I was being intentional with my time and intentional with the pursuit of my goals.

When I started Clever Girl Finance in 2015, it was born out of my personal need to create a safe space for myself and other women to talk about building wealth, our careers, and our lives. Its foundation was established from the personal blogs I had written over the years where I talked about how I was spending, saving, and investing my money, challenges I was facing as a woman at work, the side hustles I was starting, and my dating relationships (among other topics I was interested in). I shared my writing with friends and colleagues, who in turn shared it with the women in their own lives who could also relate to my experiences and challenges. These women knew exactly what I was talking about and how I was feeling, because they were feeling it, too. It wasn't initially clear to me, but Clever Girl Finance evolved from those early days of me simply sharing my thoughts and experiences.

However, if you'd told the guarded and introverted me of 2015 that my life would pivot completely and I'd be the bold female founder at the helm of one of the largest personal finance platforms for women in the US—a business so many people told me wouldn't work—I would have thought you were crazy. And while the journey was far from easy, here I am, still looking around in amazement at how far I've come.

In full honesty, when I pitched this book to my publisher, I imagined myself writing a different kind of book than the one you currently hold in your hands. It was going to be another personal finance "how-to" book, the fourth book in the Clever Girl Finance series. I thought this only made sense, considering how successful the first three were. But then my publishing editor reviewed the pitch and said, *"This is great for a future book, but I really think it's time you write about your journey. People want to know you, and you have such an important story to tell."* The response was not a surprise to me at all. In fact, I already knew it was coming. This book you're reading now, in which you'll get to learn about my story and my journey, has been a topic of conversation since my very first book pitch. But I'd consistently resisted it because, for me, it was a major challenge I wasn't quite ready to face.

For one thing, the introverted me was holding back from the discomfort of opening up. There was the fear of allowing myself to be vulnerable in telling my story. And then there was the voice in the back of my head that kept telling me that to write my story now—a story still very much in progress—would be premature. So, I made excuses and told myself that I just needed to accomplish a few more goals and reach a few more milestones, and then I would be ready to tell my story.

However, deep down, I knew I needed to write this book, and now was time to do it. I stress the word *need* because I've always known that sharing my story, my journey, my experiences was absolutely necessary, especially in a world heavily biased against women like me when it comes to wealth, business, and success. And there is value in telling a story while you're still making the journey. I learned this truth when I wrote some of my very first articles for Clever Girl Finance and got feedback from my friends and even strangers on the internet about how much they could relate to the perspective I was sharing and how much they wished the article topics were normalized conversations. After having built a platform and community, it was time to seize the opportunity to share this story I have to tell. So, I took my discomfort and fear by the collar and sat it back in the corner and told my publishing editor, *"Yes, I'll write the book now."*

Getting here has been the result of many experiences, circumstances, and realizations in my life—all of which have shaped and prepared me even though I had no idea what I was being prepared for—or that I was even preparing for anything. And even being here, by virtue of who I am and what I look like, I have found myself overlooked and undervalued countless times. I've continued to face all kinds of prejudice, sexism, and racism—but on a grander scale compared to what I was exposed to during my career days. However, the difference between the Bola back then and the Bola today is that I'm empowered, I'm bold, and I have a voice that no one can make me bury. I know who I am, and I know why I'm here.

And as I share my experiences with you on this journey of mine so far, my hope for you, the woman reading this book, is that you're inspired to tap into your greatest self, build the real wealth that you desire and deserve, and make the conscious choice to prosper, regardless of what anyone says or any circumstances that might be setting you back.

And when I say the words *wealth* and *prosper*, I'm not talking solely about money or possessions. The financial aspect of wealth is great, but don't misconstrue being wealthy and prosperous solely as having money. This is what the majority of people focus on, and in turn they miss out on so much.

The truth is, wealth and prosperity go well beyond money. I'm talking about tapping into your wealth of talent, your wealth of strength, your wealth of perseverance, and your wealth of ambition, all of which tie into and will lead you to prosperity and abundance in all areas of your life. Once you realize this, the financial side of things tends to flow more easily. Your wealth of talent allows you to hone the skills necessary to achieve whatever it is your heart desires. Your wealth of strength and perseverance allows you to follow through with your life and financial goals, especially when things get difficult. Be it achieving your greatest career heights, building the business of your dreams, improving your finances, or starting over, your wealth of ambition allows you to dream bigger than yourself and create those things. And as a result, you'll find yourself getting clear on your true purpose, which in turn will give you both an anchor and a guide to pursue living the life you deserve on your own terms. I had to realize this all for myself—and now it's your turn.

This book is for every woman who has ever been under-valued, underestimated, overlooked, or made to feel less than worthy. It's for every woman who knows she has a greater purpose and just needs the right nudges to gain clarity. It's for every woman seeking a space of relatability so she doesn't feel so alone on her business, career, and life's journey. This book is from me to you. I share my story to motivate you, empower you, and remind you that you can achieve your dreams because you are more than worthy. All you have to do is make the choice to prosper.

How to Use This Book: It's About You, Too

While the basis of this book is a reflection of my personal story and journey, it's not just about me. As I reflect on my journey so far, so will you.

At the end of each chapter, you'll find a section titled "Let's talk about you," where I'll ask you questions to help you dig deeper into your own story.

Take your time to answer and reflect on these questions. They'll help you unpack (and perhaps even uncover) parts of your past, gain clarity about your goals, and fine-tune your path to success in your career, relationships, finances, and more.

A pen and notebook would be great to help you document your reflections in the familiarity of your own handwriting and refer back to them in the future. But a notetaking app will work fine, too.

That said, let's settle in and do this.

CHAPTER 1

The Beginnings of Who I Am

Reflecting on who and what has shaped you has the power to help you craft your future.

Everyone calls me Bola for short, but my full first name is Mojibola. As with most Nigerians, I have multiple names, and my first name was given to me by my paternal grandmother. It's a name from Yoruba culture in southern Nigeria and directly translates to, *"I woke up to meet wealth."* In Yoruba, the word *wealth*, "Ola," doesn't actually refer to money. Instead, it refers to the wealth associated with joy, happiness, abundance, and well-being. In many instances, when a child is named by the Yoruba, they're named based on the prayers, hopes, and aspirations the family has for this new child. When I reflect on this, I imagine that when my grandmother named me, she had many prayers and aspirations for me, especially given the day and age she lived in.

My paternal grandmother was the only grandparent I got to know. Two of my grandparents had died long before I was born and the third died when I was only four years old. So I grew up just knowing the one grandmother whom we affectionately called "Mama."

Mama was born in 1908 and got married young. She was the fifth of the seven wives my paternal grandfather had. (Yup, my grandfather had seven wives.) Polygamous families in Nigeria were quite the norm, and my family was no exception. Culturally, polygamy had a lot to do with financial and societal status. Marriages were brokered by fathers on behalf of their daughters; the fathers either felt they were making the best decisions for their daughters or they used these marriages as opportunities for financial gain in the form of steep bride prices. For the groom, the ability to marry multiple wives and to have several children was the perfect display of this financial and societal status. However, with multiple wives and children to feed, in many instances, that display of status was short-lived.

Mama was not formally educated under the then-British colonial system that is pretty much the mainstream standard in many parts of the world today. And by "not formally educated," I mean she couldn't read or write and was considered illiterate. As she barely spoke any English, the only words she was able to say to me in English were, "good girl." She just loved to say those words to me over and over again whenever she saw me. She was a petite little lady with tribal markings on her face and traditional tattoos in green patterns covering both her arms, and she was always dressed in her traditional Buba (blouse) and Iro (wrapper). In my eyes, Mama was the sweetest grandmother ever.

My paternal grandmother, Ibidayo

As a young woman in the earlier part of the 1900s living in a small town, her expectations were to get married, be a good wife, have children (preferably male children), and care for her family. Becoming an independent woman during that time was taboo. And it was even less possible for someone who was considered illiterate. Despite this, my grandmother managed to become a successful trader in her own right, traveling to different parts of Nigeria, trading her various goods, and in turn creating an income that she used to take care of herself and her children. When she wasn't traveling around trading goods, she was working on the family farm. You may be thinking it was a family farm with tractors, an irrigation system, and animal pens, but it wasn't that kind of farm. This was a small and simple farm powered by hard work, sweat, and hand tools. The "irrigation system" was the rain that fell from the sky.

For Mama, working was a necessity. I can imagine she encountered many financial (and marital) challenges as a mother of five children, one of the youngest of seven wives, and the wife of a husband who had this huge financial obligation of providing for several other children (my paternal grandfather had 18 children in total). She was part of an extremely large family where there was not enough money to go around to take care of all the wives and children. And so, it was not uncommon for mothers in these types of family settings to get creative and find ways to earn money so they could support their own children—and that was exactly what my grandmother did with her trading business.

When going to school became an option for her children, my grandfather was against it. He did not believe in the foreign education the "colonialists" had brought to Nigeria.

He was not convinced of how it would help his children in the future. Plus, it was expensive, so off to the farm everyone went. My grandmother, on the other hand, despite her lack of education, wanted better for her children. She chose to do what she could to earn money so she could help some of her children get a formal education, despite the societal expectations that were set for her as a woman.

I remember as a teenager we would visit Mama in my dad's hometown of Oke-Mesi, a town located in the southwestern region of Nigeria in Ekiti state. It was a three- to four-hour drive from Lagos, the city we lived in. I was always excited to visit Oke-Mesi because I would get to see Mama and my dad's other siblings. At the time, Mama was well into her

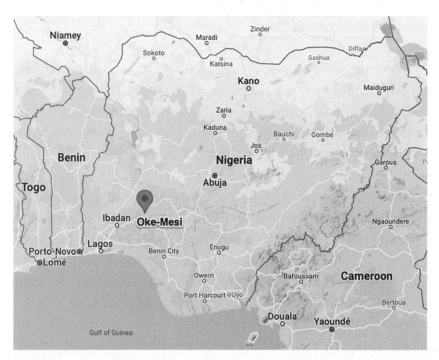

Source: maps.google.com

eighties and losing her memory. And while I didn't always understand everything she said in the dialect of Yoruba that she spoke, I would sit with her and listen to her tell me stories of her life and of people in the town.

If any of my aunties were around, they would also tell me stories of how strong Mama was and how she took care of her children. For instance, I learned that Mama gave birth to my uncle, my dad's younger brother, on her way to the family farm, which was a few miles from town and a journey she did on foot. She was with a few other women in my family, who helped her with the delivery. They found a clearing along the bush path and she gave birth right there, outside. I was told she cut the baby's umbilical cord, put him in the basket she was carrying, and then turned around and walked back home. This story blew my mind, especially when I think about how I delivered my own children—comfortably in a hospital bed with nurses, doctors, and plenty of anesthesia. This story shared by my aunties truly highlighted how strong of a woman Mama was.

I remember other times I would be visiting Mama and she would bring out these little wood carvings of her babies from decades ago who had died from one illness or the other. As she held the wood figures, she would cry profusely. I learned that it was quite common for women of her time and from our culture to have these types of carvings if they'd lost babies. She cried over these carvings all the way into her nineties because, as with any mother, she never forgot any of her children. Every time I saw her, she would always pray for me and pray for my future children. She wished me well in whatever I chose to do. Looking back, Mama was the first role model I had.

As I learned Mama's story of how she navigated her life as a young woman, one thing that became exceedingly clear to me as I visited was the big difference between my dad and his three sisters—particularly his twin sister. As a child, it just seemed normal that Mama didn't speak English and that she couldn't read or write. It also seemed normal that my dad's others sisters didn't speak English and they also couldn't read or write. But as I got older and started to realize these stark differences, I began to wonder, *Why could my dad speak English and read and write while my aunties couldn't? Why did my dad have a PhD while his twin sister didn't even have an elementary school education?*

As I began to ask questions, it became clear to me that it was because traditionally the value and expectations of the male child were not the same for the female child. If anyone was going to go to school, it would be the sons, who would later become the heads of households and decision makers in society. And the daughters—well, their expectations, much like my grandmother, were to get married, be good wives, have children (preferably male children), and care for their families. So that's just what happened. As a result, my aunties on my dad's side, in a sense, were punished by tradition.

When my grandfather finally agreed to formal education, my dad (who was 13 years old at the time) and later his younger brother, were the only ones who got to go to school, while his sisters remained at home. Today, despite the educational barrier between them, my dad and his twin sister remain best friends. But it's exceedingly clear that my aunt's life is much different from my dad's. She became a small-goods trader, traveling around the country selling her wares, just like Mama, and now lives a simple life back in their hometown.

When I see her, our conversations are full of stories, and just like Mama, she calls me "good girl," using the few English words that she knows. I often wonder what my aunt could have become if her potential had not been limited and she had had the opportunity to receive the same education as my dad.

Looking back to when I was younger, I now realize why my education and the emphasis on me doing well in school was of utmost importance to my dad. For him, education was the key to getting out of poverty and changing the trajectory of his family. His educational journey was a struggle, from starting the first grade at the age of 13 to later figuring out how to make his way to Russia with very little money during the Nigerian civil war to attend college on a scholarship. But it was all worth it.

Getting educated allowed him to pursue career opportunities he otherwise would not have had access to. It allowed him to earn money to provide for his family and to take care of his siblings. His education gave him options, and he recognized that his sisters had missed out on all of this. So he wanted his own children, especially me, his daughter, to take full advantage of every opportunity to get a good education, and he did everything within his power to ensure that my brothers and I were well educated. My mom shared his same views on education, especially for me as a female child. She wanted me to succeed more than anything.

My mom's parents were open to education regardless of gender. All my uncles and aunties had the option to go to school if they wanted to, even though money was extremely tight. My mom's oldest brother, who was a teenager by the time she started elementary school, found work and was able to help support her education. As was typical back then, my maternal grandmother was also one of many wives. And just like my paternal grandmother, she worked hard to earn money to support her children, buying and selling goods.

I unfortunately never met my maternal grandmother because she died young when my mom, Emily, was just a teenager. It was a traumatic experience for my mom. My grandmother was diabetic and was low on insulin. It wasn't something they had stocked up at home because it was extremely expensive. Unfortunately, the nearest place to get it was hours away. My mom found the money and traveled to buy the insulin. But by the time she made it back home, it was too late.

My maternal grandmother, Adebire

My mom frequently talks about her mother in admiration and about the things she had wanted to accomplish had she lived longer. She was a savvy woman who worked hard to earn her own money and put food on the table for her children, despite not having a formal education like my other grandmother. She would always talk to my mom about the importance of hard work and creating something for yourself, no matter how small. And not only did she talk about it, she put it into action herself.

My mom eventually met my dad and they got married shortly afterward. She was 19 and my dad was in his early 30s. At the time, he was about to begin a short-term teaching position at a university in the United States, so my parents moved to the United States. My oldest brother was born soon after. They moved back to Nigeria after his tenure ended and they had my two other brothers. But not too long after that, my dad got another opportunity to work as an econometrician[1] in Vienna, Austria, which is where I was born.

My parents raised my brothers and me with a heavy focus on education. As a child and young adult, my parents would always remind me why they made certain sacrifices and what having a good education could offer me. Whenever we complained about being bored, their immediate response would be, *"Go and read your books!"* While my dad's peers were buying real estate, fancy cars, and taking their entire families on summers abroad, my dad was spending the bulk

---

[1]An econometrician is an individual who uses statistics and mathematics to study, model, and predict economic principles and outcomes. https://www.investopedia.com/terms/e/econometrician.asp

of his earnings on making sure my brothers and I could go to good schools. He attached a high value to education, and so that was where he spent his money.

As I got to know more about the women in my family, I began to truly understand what the impact was of not having an education, combined with the cultural and societal pressures that women faced (and continue to face) while I was growing up. So I focused on taking full advantage of the opportunities and privilege I had, thanks to my parents' efforts.

It pains me to know that the lives of my grandmothers and aunties could have been so different. But it's also made me realize that although I cannot turn back the hands of time, I have the opportunity to succeed on their behalf. I also have the opportunity to empower my daughter and other women as well, using the knowledge I have. Every day I make the intentional choice to prosper—and these women are the early influences that shaped who I am today.

I share their stories with you to help you understand where my passion for helping women succeed comes from and why I do what I do today. I also share these stories of my upbringing to challenge you to take a look at your own history. What is your story? Who are the people in your life who set the stage and laid the path for you to be where you are right now? How does it tie into your life today? Not every story is happy-go-lucky. There may be a lot of pain, strife, and even great challenges. Some people's stories are heavier than others. But your story is your own. So how can you turn the negative aspects of your story into positives for your life today and moving forward? While you might not understand it right away, reflecting on what has shaped you has the power to help you craft your future—a better future than your past. Not just for you, but for your children, your family, and your community, too.

WHAT I'VE LEARNED

Despite the many odds that were stacked against the women in my family, they somehow managed to make life work. In my observations as a child and young adult, I not only learned about the struggles my grandmothers, my aunties, and my mom faced as women, I came to understand how my education and future success tied into their legacies. Despite not having the opportunities for themselves, they paved the way for their children and their children's children, and I am a testament of that. Learning about the sacrifices that were made for me, as the next generation, is my ultimate motivation.

LET'S TALK ABOUT YOU

Now is a good time to look back at your own family history and story, so you can see how far you've come and can reassess what you'd like to change. Here are a few questions and prompts to help you reflect:

- Take a moment to journal about your childhood. What experiences (good or bad) do you remember the most?
- Who in your family inspired you the most growing up?
- What opportunities do you wish had been available for your family?

■ What are you choosing to do better or differently to change or improve the narrative for your own future?

■ Create a one-sentence affirmation that says you deserve whatever it is you desire—financial security, a fulfilling career, healthy relationships, etc.—regardless of your past. Repeat it to yourself every day until you believe it.

Your story is important, and so is reflecting on it so you can determine the type of life you want to live. Be intentional about applying what you know, what you've learned, and what you want to do differently on your journey to crafting the future you truly desire for yourself.

CHAPTER 2

Coming of Age

Every life experience, while not always positive, is a reminder to be confident in who you are and grow thick skin.

If I were to describe my childhood, I'd describe it simply as mostly happy, with some not-so-happy moments here and there. My parents did their best to make my older brothers and me happy and comfortable but there was no denying that their marriage, as is common with many marriages, had its ups and downs as I was growing up.

By the time I was born, my mom was beginning to have several realizations about her need to make financial decisions for herself and contribute to our household financially. But by that time she was already a stay-at-home mom with four children. My parents had moved to Vienna, Austria, and my dad was working as an econometrician for OPEC (Organization of the Petroleum Exporting Countries), which was an incredible career opportunity for him. He was on an eight-year assignment from the Nigerian government and it was a major adjustment for my family, especially my mom, who was living in a new country, learning a new language, and facing many prejudices.

As a toddler and little kid, I was too young to remember certain things. And what I did remember, I was too little to understand until much later. There were, however, some memories that have always stayed with me. I remember sticking my foot in the space between the elevator and floor level in our apartment building as a four-year-old, only to have my entire leg (rainboot and all) get stuck there. I remember my mom panicking and the emergency services coming and taking what felt like 10 hours to set my foot free. I thought it was funny for the first 30 seconds, until I realized what I'd done. I have a permanent scar on my right foot that reminds me of that day.

There were other stories my older brothers would share with me of things that happened before I was born or when I was baby. There was the story about the night my dad parked his car on the street as always in our all-white neighborhood and the next morning he went outside, ready to head to work, only to find the car mounted on concrete blocks, with the tires stacked next to it and a note that said, *"Your family isn't welcome here."* There was also the time my oldest brother, while legally crossing the street in a crosswalk, was intentionally hit and injured by a driver who then proceeded to speed off without stopping to check on the child he had hit.

My parents fortunately had the support of the Nigerian expatriate community in Vienna to lean on as they navigated life there. They made friends and created a life for themselves. My dad stayed busy at work while my mom dealt with school prep, homework, and after-school activities with my brothers and a baby (me). It was around this time, after I was born, that my mom decided she wanted to do more for herself. She had made friends within the Nigerian community and had started to see things happening around her that made her uncomfortable. She was seeing friends unable to leave bad relationships, friends who had unfortunately lost their spouses, and friends who were unable to make or participate in key decisions in their homes. While other factors could have been at play, one consistent theme with many of her friends was that they didn't have access to or even know much about their family finances. And as a result, they had limited to no options when it came to making major well-being and life decisions.

Around the same time that my mom was making all these observations and coming to her realizations, one of her closest friends at the time committed suicide. She was devasted. And while what happened is not something I can personally elaborate on, being that I was so young and it is also not my story to share, I can imagine this was a major catalyst in the decision my mother made to seek more for herself. Starting with her decision to go back to school so she could secure her future by getting her college degree. To her, going to school to get a college degree was a gateway to potential opportunities that would give her options. It would allow her to contribute to our family finances and support herself if she needed to.

The idea of my mom going back to school at that particular time, however, was not something my dad was keen on, and as a child I remember them having many arguments. From my dad's perspective, it could have been that he felt like she was challenging his ability to take care of his family by feeling that she needed to get her college degree so she could also get a well-paying job. There was also the question of the kids and who would take care of us. Perhaps he felt she could have waited until my brothers and I were older to make it easier. There was a lot of tension in my parents' marriage around this time, but my mom was unrelenting about going back to school. I remember attending college classes with her, us sitting down in the back of the classroom and her telling me to be as quiet as possible. I remember it being really hard to stay quiet.

I was also right there with her when she decided to move to Albany, New York, with the money she had saved to obtain

With my mom on her college campus on our way to class

a secretarial certification that she could add on to her college degree. (She left my three older brothers under my dad's care during this time.) I can never forget our tiny little basement apartment in that undesirable part of town and the guest roaches we had because that was all she could afford with her meager savings.

I was also right there at her college graduation, staring in amazement as she walked across the podium to accept her degree. When I reflect back on those memories, I realize how incredibly impactful that particular moment was on me—my

My mom's graduation

mom graduating from college and I somehow knowing it was a big deal, even though I was so young. To me, my mom was Superwoman and the applause from the audience was just for her because she was so amazing. I was so proud.

Not long after my mom got her college degree and additional certification, she went on to get a master's degree. Shortly afterward, my dad's work assignment in Vienna ended and my family moved back to Nigeria.

My mom hit the ground running. She started out working full-time at an investment bank and at the same time began setting up multiple businesses. She had a Coca-Cola franchise, a bakery, a hair salon, and even started a girl's school. As time went on, she hired people to work at her businesses and was there overseeing things in the evenings after her full-time job and on the weekends. She was the ultimate side-hustle queen.

Given the economic situation in Nigeria, having a side hustle alongside your main hustle was pretty much the norm. Everyone was doing it to create additional streams of income and to establish some type of financial security, given the uncertainty of jobs and the economy as a whole. Still, it was challenging for my mom to balance kids, the household, her full-time job, and her businesses all at the same time, even with help at home, so she eventually left her corporate job to pursue her businesses full time.

As for me, I settled into primary (grade) school, which was a tough transition for me initially because I started getting teased for having a German accent. But in a matter of time, my German accent disappeared and I settled into school life just fine as "one of the kids," and no longer as "the kid with the German accent." I made friends in my neighborhood and was a carefree kid, living my best life while getting myself into lots of trouble.

After school I would run off to play with the kids in my neighborhood, and half the time I would come back with a bruise or a cut. Once my friends and I crawled under a fence at a local construction site where fresh cement had just been poured. Oblivious to what I was doing, I dipped both my hands into it. While I pulled my hands out quickly, it didn't take long for what was left of the cement to start burning my skin. I ran home crying, and my mom, seeing the trouble I'd gotten myself into, started crying, too. It was a terrible evening at the ER having those cement burns treated.

Usually, once summer break came around, my mom would pack our bags and she and I would go off to her hometown, Ibillo, which was located in the southwestern part of Nigeria in Edo state and a five-hour drive from Lagos.

As a child, the times I spent there were some of the best times of my childhood, even though it wasn't surrounding the best circumstances. My six cousins and I would spend all day running around the farm my Aunty Kike owned with

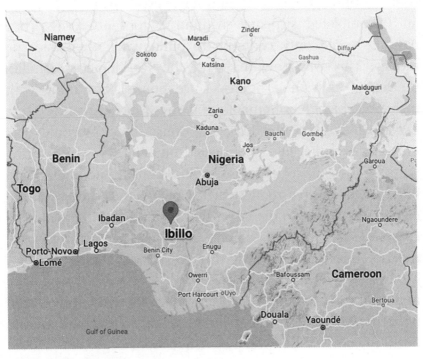

Source: maps.google.com

her husband, eating the cashews and guavas we picked from the trees, running away from fire ants, and climbing up trees we had no business climbing. But we loved it. To me, I was there purely to have fun. However, in reality, my mom took all the time she could each summer break to go back to her hometown to visit and help her family.

Aunty Kike was my mom's younger sister, and she worked as a teacher in the local primary school. Her husband also worked in education doing administrative duties, and together they used the savings from their meager salaries to purchase the couple of acres where they had their farm.

They had started building a modest home on the land as well, but money was tight, and for over 20 years it remained an uncompleted structure without a roof or doors. They basically could only continue to build when they had the money. This was how many of the working-class families in Nigeria built their homes, since home loans came with incredibly high requirements and my aunt and uncle were not eligible. As young kids, my cousins and I would play hide-and-seek in the uncompleted building. Prior to starting work on their main house, my aunt and uncle had managed to build a smaller three-room structure next to the house where all eight of them lived in the hopes that their main house would be completed someday. And whenever my mom and I arrived from the city, there would be 10 of us there in those three rooms.

My aunt and her family didn't mind. In fact, my aunt would do everything she could to make us as comfortable as she possibly could. Whenever we visited from Lagos, she would stretch herself thin and go above and beyond her means to make sure everything was perfect by buying expensive food items she would never buy for her own family because she didn't want my mom to worry about how she was doing. She would walk the half mile or so to the market to buy these items or have my uncle give her ride on his old motorcycle. They didn't own a car because they couldn't afford one. On more than one occasion as we made our arrival into town, we'd see my aunt walking hurriedly from the market with her heavy bags, rushing home to get things ready before we arrived. We'd of course pull over and she would reluctantly get in the car, disappointed that we'd caught her before she got home to prepare for our arrival. My mom would get upset because she knew my aunt couldn't afford all the things she'd bought. But my aunt was stubborn and so she did it anyway. That was Aunty Kike, generous to a fault and always putting everyone's needs before her own. She was always reluctant to ask my mom for help, but my mom helped her sister out however she could.

Aunty Kike in her early twenties

Unfortunately, my aunt became ill and died while she was still in her forties, leaving her young children behind. My aunt, as always, didn't want to give my mom another thing to worry about so she never revealed the true extent of her illness or how much help she really needed until it was too late. She died because they did not have enough money to get the medical care and surgery she desperately needed. In Nigeria, health insurance is not something that's even an option for most people. And if you fall sick, it comes at a cost that needs to be paid entirely out of pocket—many times even before any medical services are rendered. And so, as a result of this high cost, many people tend to seek out less-expensive traditional healing remedies, which my aunt also did. My mom was devastated because, living five hours away, she wasn't fully aware of how sick her sister was. Had she known, she would have done everything she could to help her sister. The death of my aunt was an extremely painful loss in my family, and my mom often reflects on the tragedy that took her from us.

As a child, there are many things you don't understand. But even at that young age, I realized that not having the financial means to afford something could have a devastating impact on a family. However, as I got older, I also realized that despite what my aunt and uncle didn't have, the time we spent with them each summer and the experiences that came with that time were full of happiness. From running around with my cousins and laughing so hard until my belly hurt, to watching my mom and aunt make dinner while teasing each other about who was the better cook, to the whole family sitting outside late into the night just talking—these are things that money could never buy. That happiness and those memories will last forever in my mind.

A few years later, I was in high school and it was time to start thinking about college. My dad had spent a significant amount of his income on tuition for my older brothers (first for boarding school abroad, then later on college in the United States, supplementing whatever student loans they were able to qualify for with relatives as co-signers). Given my dad's upbringing, giving his children a good education was something he prioritized. And no matter the cost, he was going to do everything he could to ensure his children got the best education possible.

However, around the same time I started thinking about college, my family was also going through a series of financial transitions. While my mom was now working full time with her businesses, my dad was forced to retire about 15 years earlier than he had planned due to downsizing in his workplace and then health issues.

In the grand scheme of one's financial and retirement planning, 15 years is a big deal. And given that he earned a significant portion of the household income, there were some major changes to the way we lived, as the money my mom was earning was not enough to support our entire family. So we downsized. We went from owning three cars to just one. We moved from our five-bedroom, two-garage house to a small, three-bedroom apartment in a cheaper neighborhood, and the flow of money in our household got much tighter. Being a teenager, my mind exaggerated everything that was happening. And so to me, life as I knew it was over forever. I remember my dad sitting me down to tell me there was no way he could afford my college tuition abroad, and as a non-US citizen, I didn't qualify for student loans without a US co-signer. At this time, our relatives in the US had already helped to co-sign student loans for my brothers, so my parents didn't feel comfortable asking them again. I was disappointed.

At this time, Nigeria was going through a lot of economic instability, which trickled down into the education system. There were constant professor strikes at public universities and several months at a time where these schools were closed. Private universities were rare, so that was not even an option. I remember my college-aged cousins being home for nine months without any classes due to one of these long strikes. Their university then opened for a couple of months, only to close down again for another six months. I could feel their frustration, with the average four-year degree now being extended into six or seven years due to the strikes.

I had already taken the Nigerian University entrance exams and was narrowing down schools to apply to when my parents came up with an idea. Instead of looking at schools in the US, I could look at going to college in Vienna, where I was born. My mother had thought through her finances and figured that she could help me with the financial cost of going to college there instead if we had some help with my accommodation costs. My parents had close friends who lived there, and in discussing the possibility of me going to college in Vienna with them, they offered to let me stay at their home without any hesitation whatsoever. In fact, my Aunty Winnie and Uncle Muazu wouldn't even hear of me staying in the college dorms. Their generosity was an incredible cost savings for my parents, and so the decision was made. I would apply to my mother's alma mater in Vienna, Webster University.

Upon getting accepted, my parents sat me down to set their expectations with me; my mom was sending me to college at the expense of her own personal goals and my parents' retirement plans. She let me know that the fact that she was paying for my college education was a privilege and not my right. So in return she expected me to stay focused, get good grades, and seek out opportunities for scholarships if at all possible. She also told me to remember where I came from, to be proud of who I was, and to never let anyone take advantage of me. Personally, I did not take this opportunity lightly. I knew the cost at which it came, and so my goal was to make my parents proud.

In Vienna, my aunt and uncle welcomed me and treated me like their own daughter and made me as comfortable as possible even when I felt homesick. Aunty Winnie helped me get set up with my college classes. And although school was an hour away from their home, she came with me on my first few commutes to school on the bus and train to make sure I didn't get lost on my own. School, on the other hand, was certainly an adjustment.

Webster University is a large international American university with its main campus in St. Louis, Missouri. But the Vienna campus, at the time I was there, was very small, with only about 350 students in attendance. For the first two semesters, I was the only black student on campus until one other student arrived and we became fast friends. We were the only two until I left. I was surrounded by a lot of rich kids who came from different parts of Europe and the Middle East. They came to school in their BMWs and Audis, and I was the only one I knew who rode the bus and train.

There were students who were genuinely interested in learning about my background and where I was from. And then there were the students who were just ignorant and made assumptions about who I was before they even got to know me. When they spoke to me, I was asked questions about how I managed to make it to Vienna and if I'd ever been on an airplane before. I was asked if they could touch my hair and if my father was a king of a jungle in Africa. I was asked how I could afford to attend college there, all the way from Africa.

One particularly ignorant girl and her friends came up to me one day asking me a similar line of questions, saying she heard the journey from Africa was such a long one and she wanted to know what the experience was like for me. So, I decided to indulge her. I told her the journey was incredibly difficult, and as a matter of fact, I had trekked for two weeks from Lagos to Cairo, Egypt. When I got to Cairo, I took a boat on the Nile all the way to Turkey, and when I got to Turkey, I got on a plane for the first time in my life and, well . . . there I was. Her response to my ridiculous story was, *"Wow! No wonder you Africans don't like to travel!"* Then after a few seconds of reflection, she said, *"Wait, is that really a true story?"* and my response to her and her friends was an eye roll and then a blank stare. She got the message. But then as she turned to leave with her friends, I decided I could be the bigger person and chose to educate her instead. So I told her:

> *Actually, Africa is not a country. It is an entire continent with 54 countries. I come from one of those countries called Nigeria.*

*No, you can never ever touch my hair and in the
context that you asked, that's actually an extremely
rude question.*

*And just like you weren't raised in a jungle, neither was
I, and neither is my father the king of said jungle.*

That wasn't the first or the last time I would get asked
ridiculous questions about being African. But then I also
realized I didn't have to indulge anyone's ignorance, and I
also didn't need to play into it, either.

There was that type of ignorance—the kind that made you
want to roll your eyes and question a person's thought
process—and then there was the direct racism. As a child,
my experiences with racism were not something I dwelt on
because I didn't fully grasp what it meant. But as a young
adult now in college, I was fully aware of what racism was,
and the experiences I faced always put me on high alert.
My experiences with racism in Vienna were direct and
straightforward. There was no niceness or politeness about
it. There was no beating around the bush. It always clear and
very evident:

*We cannot be friends because you are black.
I don't like you, because you are black.
You are black, so I don't want you here.*

I experienced grown adults making monkey sounds when
I walked by. On several occasions, I'd sit next to someone on
a bus or train, only to have them get up and move to another
seat or stay standing, shooting me dagger eyes in the process.

In later years, upon my reflection of my experiences with racism in America, I would find a contrast. In America, I found that racism is polite and disrespectful, subtle and harsh, all at the same time. It's like the neighbor I had in Philadelphia when I had gotten married who would compliment me on my outfit whenever she saw me but called the cops to report "strangers that made her uncomfortable" when my brother, niece, and nephews visited me and I took them to the apartment complex swimming pool as my guests. It's like the cop who recently tailgated my husband in our predominately white neighborhood and then pulled him over close to our house, only to politely ask him, *"Sir, how are you doing today?"* and then follow up with, *"Why are you in this neighborhood?"* in an equally polite manner. And while these different contrasts in racism exist, both types are disgusting and I'm not sure which of the two is more dangerous.

But back to Vienna. I vividly remember one Christmas Day when my friend (the only other black person from my university) invited me to her parents' house to spend the day with them, since my family was in Nigeria and my aunt and uncle were away visiting their kids abroad for the holidays. Her parents had moved their family from Uganda to Vienna for a job opportunity and we'd become close friends. She was already out in town, so our plan was to meet up and then ride the Strassenbahn (street train) together to where she lived with her family. We were excited to hang out. It was Christmas Day, the weather was bright and sunny, and we had a lot to talk about on the train.

My friend and I were talking and laughing when all of a sudden, a voice came from behind and said in German what translated into, *"I don't know why you are so happy when you are just a couple of Niggers."* I turned around to face a young white man looking at us and laughing. It was clear that he had been drinking. But in that moment, I was overcome with so much anger that I rolled up the magazine I had in my hand, and even though my friend tried to stop me, I started to hit him with it as hard as I could. I also realized in that moment that my actions were not particularly smart. He could have easily overpowered me if he had wanted to and even caused me serious harm. Luckily for me, he didn't hit back. Instead, he tried to grab onto the magazine I was hitting him with while he continued to hurl racist abuses at us. The train driver noticed the ruckus in his rearview mirror and pulled the train to an emergency stop.

With us being "black," the obvious assumption was that the driver was either getting ready to throw us off the train or call the police. And so, I forgot all about the nuisance racist and instead my friend and I quickly started to gather our belongings in preparation to get thrown off the train as the driver angrily walked back to where we were sitting. To our surprise, he grabbed the man who had been insulting us by his coat collar, hit the button to open the train doors, and threw him out onto the sidewalk. Then, he turned to us and said he'd heard everything. He apologized to us and told us to take our seats.

Thinking back on that incident, there are so many ways the situation could have gone wrong. I was angry and I felt powerless. The only thing I thought I could do was use my fists. But what if that guy had actually beaten me up? What if he had a knife? What if the train driver had instead decided to call the police on me? I wasn't sorry for what I did (and I'm still not), but I was afraid of the fact that my outburst could have had serious consequences—and then what would I have told my parents? That I was fighting with an idiot who was irrelevant to my life on the train? I told myself that was the last time I would let someone else's stupidity and ignorance potentially jeopardize any opportunities my parents and I had worked so hard for.

And then there was Andreas. Andreas was a blue-eyed, blonde-haired gorgeous Austrian boy who attended college with me. I met him one day in between classes, and although we had completely different majors and didn't share any classes, we hit it off pretty quickly. He would walk with me to my classes before going to his. We would meet up for lunch and hang out in the rec room to play foosball. And while we were not dating, we had become really good friends, and there were definitely butterflies.

A couple months into our friendship, Andreas showed up to the rec room not looking like himself. Not too long after he came in, he said we needed to talk. I couldn't imagine what he had to say; maybe he wasn't doing well in class? Maybe something happened at home? I was worried about him. But as he spoke, my worry quickly turned into irritation, and then into annoyance.

He said he had brought up our friendship to some of his friends because he had started to have feelings for me. But after hearing what his friends had to say and thinking through things himself, he realized that dating, or even staying friends, was not realistic because. . .well. . .I was black. And so maybe we could just be cool. I couldn't believe my ears. What was unrealistic about being friends with or dating a black person? What did "just be cool" even mean? I was not raised to consider someone's race before I decided if we could be friends or even date, so his reasoning did not make sense to me. In those moments as he was speaking, I even tried to see the logic in his statements because I thought that maybe I had misunderstood something he'd said. But then I immediately got mad at myself for even considering that the nonsense coming out of his mouth had any logic whatsoever, which made me even angrier. He'd just said we couldn't be friends because I was black!

And so, I told Andreas, without mincing my words, that despite how nice he seemed as a human being, the fact that the deciding factor of whether we could be friends was based on my skin color and the fact that he'd decided our friendship was "unrealistic," again, based on my skin color, meant that he was a racist. I told him no, we could *not* be cool. In fact, we would never be cool: Why would I want to be cool with a racist? I let him know that I would never allow his ignorance or anyone else's to make me feel less than I am because I am black, and he needed to do some serious soul searching and lose some friends. I then dared him to ever look my way again if he knew what was good for him. If I showed up somewhere, he needed to leave. If he saw me in the hallways or on the streets, he needed to turn around and walk the other way. His face turned into an expression of shocked horror, and then he tried to apologize. Clearly, he wasn't expecting my response. But what other kind of response did he really think he would get? That I would say, *"Oh, okay. I understand"*? Yeah, I'm not the one. The next time Andreas saw me on campus, he turned around and walked the other way.

While not always positive, these experiences shaped me. Each one reminded me to be confident about who I was and where I come from—and very importantly, to grow thick skin. There were, however, also several good things about my college experience. For instance, I was fortunate to get two partial scholarships based on my grades, in exchange for working in the computer lab and in the library. This covered a significant portion of my tuition while I was in Vienna. As email became more mainstream, working at the computer lab gave me the opportunity to keep in touch with friends from high school who had either stayed in Nigeria or, like me, moved abroad for college. I had access to a computer and uninterrupted internet, and so I spent my time sending emails and exploring the "World Wide Web" when I wasn't helping out other students. I also certainly took full advantage of my job at the library and spent hours photocopying chapters of available textbooks in advance of my classes so I wouldn't have to buy them. This saved me a ton of money on the expensive textbooks I needed.

There was also the amazing experience of meeting one of my mom's old college professors, Professor Boch, who would tell me every time she saw me that she could swear she knew me from somewhere but couldn't quite place it. She would say, *"I know I've said this to you before, but you somehow seem familiar to me. . .it's like I know you."* I had no clue what she was talking about and each time she mentioned it, I would tell her I didn't think we had met before. I didn't think much of it until weeks into the semester, when I was telling my mom about how my classes were going. I randomly mentioned the professor's name and my mom said, *"Wait, say that name again."* Come to find out, Professor Boch taught one of the classes my mom took me to as a three- or four-year-old, when we'd sit at the back of the class. When I told Professor Boch, she exclaimed,

"I knew we had met!" She remembered my mom and me as a little girl in her class. She said that my mom was extremely bold, given the time. And while some professors complained about having a child in their classrooms, she didn't mind because she understood the sacrifice as a mother and she knew my mom was going to do what it took to succeed. Hearing those words not only made me proud of my mom but also reminded me even more about the efforts she had made to set the stage for me in my own life—and it motivated me to do well in school.

My classes, while sometimes challenging, went well, and I got through them getting mostly As and a few Bs, with the exception of one particular computer science class called Data Structures and Algorithms. It was a class I didn't particularly like, and it didn't help that the professor was mean. He told us from the start that the class would be hard and half of us would fail it, and true to his prediction, half of us did—including me. The class was a struggle, and my final grade was a big fat D (Poor). As a result, my GPA (grade-point average) fell to 3.4 and I was terrified of telling my mom, knowing how hard she was working to help me get through school. Looking back, a 3.4 GPA was still pretty good but, in that moment, when I got my grade, I was devastated. All I could think of was that the thousands of dollars my mom had spent paying for this class had gone down the drain. I cried and cried, and then decided I would tell no one. Not even my mom. I then reregistered for the class with a different instructor and made the passing grade to take the next class. My overall GPA was still affected but I had passed the class. For some reason, my parents didn't ask me about how that particular class went, so I didn't have to tell them anything. However, getting a poor grade in another class was not an option, and it did not happen again. (Dear Mommy, if you are reading this: I love you and hey, I still turned out okay, right?)

My junior year, I had the opportunity to do an exchange program for a semester at my college's London campus. One of my best friends lived nearby, so I stayed with her and her family while I went to class. I loved every moment of being in London because so many of my high school friends had gone to college in the UK and I got to see them all the time. It felt like home and it was a great experience to pass the time, as I missed my family, especially my mom.

By that time, my mom had moved back to the States and was working odd jobs to earn enough money to help me with my tuition while she pursued a nursing degree. Things were tight, and seeing how much she was working, I wanted to do something to ease the strain. I had started my immigration process and moved to the US just before my last year of college. Although my parents were against it, I decided to take a year off from college to work and give my mother a much-needed financial break.

During my "gap year," I also happened to stumble across an Avon catalog and quickly signed up to become an Avon sales rep. I made it a point to sell the products to every single one of my mom's friends and other women I met. A lot of my mom's friends loved the Avon cream pots and were already buying them from other people, so once they knew I was an "Avon girl" they were happy to switch over and become my customers. They would pay for their orders in advance and then wait for their deliveries that would arrive a couple weeks later. This was great, because it allowed me to order the products from the catalog using the payments I received, since I had no starting capital.

I also got a job close to home as a data entry clerk. I hated that job and the work environment, but it allowed me to work 40 hours a week at $10 an hour. I saved all the money I earned to put toward school, to host a bridal shower for my now sister-in-law, and to buy my plane tickets to and from the wedding.

I went back to college the next school year, going to the Webster University home campus in St. Louis, Missouri, which allowed for a much easier transition, since I'd already been attending their Vienna campus. I lived on campus in the apartment housing. In some ways, going to school in St. Louis was very reminiscent of school in Vienna. For instance, next door to me, there was a girl who drove a lime green Mercedes drop-top convertible with a silver frame around her license plate that said, *"Daddy bought it, guess who got it."* A car for me, on the other hand, was out of the question, so I walked and rode the bus everywhere. I also managed to get a job on campus for a few hours a week updating the volleyball team's website and getting paid $116 every two weeks. I told my mom I had a job so she could stop sending me pocket money, and I stretched my paycheck as far and as hard as I could to buy groceries, pay my cell phone bill, and do other small things. My roommate worked at the student center and she would always let me know when there was free food, which helped supplement my meager grocery budget.

I couldn't have been happier when graduation came around. It meant I could finally go home to my mom, who at this time had become a U.S. citizen and now lived and worked in New Jersey as a nurse. She was traveling back and forth to Lagos every few months to see my dad, who also visited the States often. Graduation meant that the massive financial obligation of paying for college was over, and my mom was thrilled to be done. My dad flew to St. Louis from Nigeria to attend my graduation while my mom stayed in New Jersey to save on costs. They were both incredibly proud of me. I successfully graduated with a Bachelor of Science in Computer Science and a minor in Business.

All in all, I am grateful for my college experience. Everything I experienced, both positive and negative, helped me prepare for my journey as an adult in the real world. As a young woman, college set the stage for me to build confidence and start learning how to stand up for myself, especially as a black woman. It helped me navigate a variety of emotions that in turn would influence how I chose to respond or react to similar situations in the future. It was foundational to my personal growth. And leaning on the advice of my parents, I chose to take every experience as a learning opportunity for what to do differently or better the next time I was faced with a challenge. And as we all know, and as I would continue to learn, life is full of challenges.

WHAT I'VE LEARNED

Watching my mom make the decision to get a college education and as a result be able to contribute to our household finances in the way that she did gave me the first taste of what having financial independence as woman could really mean. I watched my mom stand up for herself to pursue her dreams and in turn create opportunities for me. And while it took me a while to find my own footing when I first started college, away from my friends and family, it was there that I truly developed my sense of self, started learning how to stand up for myself, and understood my worth. Each memorable experience I had in college, including the waves of emotions I felt, contributed immensely to my personal growth as a young adult.

LET'S TALK ABOUT YOU

Sometimes certain experiences happen that might make you question who you are or challenge your values. In the moment, you might feel all kinds of emotions, but upon reflection, there are always lessons to learn that can help shape the future you.

Let's go back to some of your earlier days when you were in college or high school and unpack some of those experiences. Here are some questions to help you reflect.

- What financial challenges affected you and your family?
- What experiences did you have that helped you build grit or allowed you to come to certain realizations? What were those realizations?
- How can you leverage what you learned from those challenges and personal experiences as a young adult to fuel your personal growth?

We all have those memories, both pleasant or otherwise, from our high school and college days (and even throughout our lives). As you reflect on yours, focus on how those memories have shaped you and lay out the life lessons you learned from your experiences that you can apply to your personal growth today.

CHAPTER 3

My Career Journey

Don't be afraid to be bold on your career path. It might take practice as you step into your own, but remember your self-worth.

Once I graduated from college, going to graduate school was not even a consideration for me. In fact, it was the very last thing on my mind. While friends would talk to me about where they planned to go to grad school for a master's degree or MBA, my main priority was finding a job after graduation and finding one fast. As soon as I got home to New Jersey where my mom was, I started applying to any and every kind of job. I figured that if it took me a while to find a corporate job, I could still make money by working odd jobs. So, while I was applying to technology and business jobs, I was also applying to jobs at the local mall and at local businesses to work as a cashier or salesperson. It didn't take long for me to find a job as a photo lab technician and cashier at my local CVS pharmacy.

I was paid minimum wage, and since I still didn't own a car, I would put on my CVS polo shirt and walk the 20 minutes or so to work just before it was time for my shift. As a photo lab technician, I learned how to process and develop camera film (back when digital cameras were still ridiculously expensive)—and let me tell you, I saw all kinds of things on the film I developed, both appropriate and otherwise. On one occasion, I even had to get my manager to step in to calm down an angry customer who had violated store policy by trying to get some extremely explicit images printed. I was so distraught by the customer's behavior in the store that I was ready to quit that job right then and there. Fortunately for me, I had successfully gotten through the interview process and got my first corporate job at one of the big-three US consulting firms at the time, so I didn't have to stick around for long.

Working in consulting was exciting. I was hired as a technology and strategy consultant, and it was my first real job. I was earning more money than I'd ever earned in my entire life. My base pay was $54,000 before taxes, and you couldn't tell me anything. As far as I was concerned, I was rich. I would soon find out, however, that living in the New York City metro area was not cheap, and that feeling of being rich dissipated as fast as it came.

I threw myself into my new job, traveling all over the country working on different projects and for different technology clients doing everything from coding to quality assurance testing to strategy development and implementation. Working as a consultant was very fast paced, which kept me very busy. Plus, I was learning a lot. I was so happy to have a job and to be earning money. So happy, in fact, that it never occurred to me to negotiate my salary or even ask for a sign-on bonus before I signed my contract. My assumption was that I had to take what I was given—otherwise it would be taken away. How to negotiate my salary wasn't something I had discussed with my parents, and none of my friends were talking about their salaries, either, so I was pretty much oblivious to the fact that doing this was even an option. I just took the salary that was offered to me and that was it.

As time went by, I got to know my work colleagues and became friends with some of them. One day over lunch, we randomly started discussing our job roles and how much we were each earning, despite the fact that HR would not have been too happy about the conversation if they were to find out. As the conversation progressed, I realized that another colleague and I were the lowest earners at the table, despite the fact that all of us were hired into similar positions and we all had similar educational backgrounds. During our conversation, I learned that some of my work colleagues made thousands of dollars more than I did, and some of them even got sign-on bonuses. The reason why they were earning more? Well, unlike me, they didn't accept the first offer they received. Instead, they asked for more.

Not only did asking for more get them more money, but it also positioned them to earn more in terms of raises and bonuses over the life of their career at the company because these raises and bonuses were given as a percentage of their base salary. And while I didn't make it apparent to my colleagues, I was shocked and disappointed. Not at anyone else, but at myself. I was mad at my ignorance and at the opportunity I had missed out on to earn more. I was so disappointed in myself that at the next meeting I had with my career counselor from work, I made it a point to bring it up to ask for advice. At the time, every junior employee was assigned a career counselor who was at the executive level of the company to get guidance and mentorship. Meetings happened every few months and were confidential. The best part of having a career counselor was that if you had a great connection with them, the relationship could be invaluable.

My first career counselor was a woman named Claudia, and upon sharing my grievances about my pay with her, she told me to schedule a meeting with my manager to discuss what I'd need to accomplish over the next few months performance-wise to receive the highest-tier raise and bonus when that time came around. This was one way I could try to make up for not negotiating my salary at the beginning. Her advice was incredibly helpful. Not only did I have the conversation with my manager to set expectations, I met and exceeded those expectations and was able to get a decent raise and bonus at the top tier. And although my raises and bonuses at the company could have been higher if I had negotiated my base salary to begin with (since they were calculated as a percentage of my base salary), I took it as a learning experience. That was the last time I would be leaving money on the table.

In fact, with every promotion or new job, I would lay out my negotiation strategy in advance. I would highlight the immense value I was bringing to the company or position based on my skillset and experience, what I planned to accomplish, and how I planned to do it. I got so good at negotiating my salary that at the final job I had before I left corporate America to run my business full time, I not only negotiated my salary, my sign-on bonus, and my potential first year's raise, but I also negotiated my vacation days from two weeks to three weeks, my computer from a basic HP to a MacBook Pro, and I got my employer to upgrade my standard office chair to one that was ergonomically more comfortable. These negotiations did not happen all at once, though. Instead, I brought them up at the appropriate times throughout my hiring and onboarding process. And if there's one piece of advice I can give you as a woman, it's this: get comfortable negotiating, knowing your worth, and owning it—that's exactly what I did.

At work, I continued to learn how to stand up for myself as I worked on the different consulting projects I was assigned to and as a female employee. I remember one time I was working on an intense high-profile project that was of top priority to our client's senior management. My team was small and the work was intense. Our client had an extremely large customer base and their system has a lot of moving pieces. Being the most junior person on the team at the time, I found myself being assigned the bulk of the grunt work that no one else wanted to do. I didn't complain, though. I came in early, stayed late, and delivered my work above and beyond expectations. I was in the office for the 1 a.m. to 7 a.m. test cycle shifts where we ran specific system tests late at night based on different test plans to ensure the system was performing as expected, I worked the 12-hour days troubleshooting different system issues, and I delivered without complaint.

Once a week, there was a leadership status update meeting where the status of our project was shared with the client's senior executives. I'd never attended this meeting, as I'd never been invited (our team updates were provided by our team lead and our manager). One day, however, I ran into one of the client executives at lunch and in speaking briefly about the project, he said he'd love to hear my take on how things were going so I should attend one of the next meetings. At work, I personally preferred to stay in my comfort zone where I didn't have to present anything or get asked any questions from senior executives that I wasn't sure I knew how to answer. As an introvert, this client request was the last thing I wanted to do. But I realized it could be an opportunity to gain visibility not just from the clients but from my own manager as well. So, I told my team lead that I'd like to attend the meeting. He initially had a lot of hesitation and made excuses about how it wasn't necessary for me to be there. He even told me that the conference room was too small for an extra person. But once I told him I had been asked to attend by the client, he had no choice but to let me come. The meeting ran for 90 minutes and was in a conference room that had plenty of space. During this time the various teams working on the project presented their updates and answered any questions. When it came our team's turn to present, my team lead immediately took over, providing all the updates even when questions were directed at me. I could barely get a word in because he was answering for me and talking over me. What was most shocking were the updates he was providing. He took credit for all my ideas, discoveries, and hard work. He explained everything I had shared with him about my work like he was the one who'd done it or come up with the idea. From the critical issues I'd discovered, to my suggested ideas on how to resolve them, to my process improvements suggestions, he took credit for it all.

I left the meeting furious. I was so angry that I didn't even go back to my desk right away. As I walked around the office building, I realized I needed to create a plan, because having an angry outburst at my team lead was not the way to go. It could backfire and give him an opportunity to sabotage my performance reviews (and in turn my job), since he provided feedback about my role to our project manager. I also didn't want to make him feel like he had the upper hand or that he had gotten to me. So, I decided right there and then that while I would continue to work with him, I would document all my status updates, ideas, and discoveries. And as opposed to telling them to him verbally, I would create a weekly email where I would not only copy my manager but the rest of our small team working on the project as well.

When my first update email went out, my team lead came to me almost immediately to ask why I had sent it. I responded politely, saying I wanted to keep everyone up to date on what I was working on. I could see the annoyance on his face, even though he tried to hide it. His days of taking credit for my work were done. I'd made sure of it. I sent that email each and every week until my role on that project concluded and I categorized them under "boss moves" in my career experience folder. I was proud of how I handled the situation. And this approach of sending a weekly status email (whether I was asked to or not) became part of my personal standard operating procedures because I knew that type of team lead was not going to be the last one I encountered.

I was typically the youngest person on my projects and in the technology industry as a whole, working with clients who had been on the job several years. I was also usually the only woman (or one of a couple). Most of the time, I was able to handle any issues on my own. For instance, when a client made a joke at a meeting and called me the "office baby," I politely told him why I was qualified to be there. There was also the time a client got upset that the data I was presenting in a meeting conflicted with his own. He said, *"I've been working here since before you were born; I know what I'm talking about."* I simply and politely referred him to the reliable data sources I'd used to validate my own results.

As I began to gain experience in my career, I realized that work aggravations were inevitable—there was bound to be someone who would annoy me or criticize me or try to embarrass or diminish me. And so as opposed to getting upset or having angry outbursts, my mantra was to kill them with kindness every single time. And that's exactly what I did, and I did it very well, too.

There were, however, instances where I needed an advocate at work to support me during some uncomfortable experiences on the projects I was working on. For instance, there was the time I had been assigned to a new client project, and a couple weeks into it one of the senior executives asked me to schedule a meeting with him to go over some updates. I did it without hesitation because after all, my team worked for him. It wasn't until I sat down in his office and began to cover my updates that I realized his true intentions. He was completely disinterested in the information I was sharing. Instead, the questions revolved around my personal life, including whether I was single and if I would like to go to dinner with him, all while the photos of his wife and kids sat on the table in his office. It was extremely uncomfortable and I tried to keep the conversation on the topic of work, but he wouldn't relent. Each time I changed the topic to focus on the updates, he would go right back to probing me about my personal life, so I excused myself.

I went straight to my desk and sat down to think about what happened. I was bothered by the fact that he had asked me on a date. While there were many office relationships going on and it wasn't against any company policies, my issue was that he was clearly married—and despite my obvious discomfort in his office, he wouldn't stop pressing. Plus, he was much older than me, which made it even more intimidating. I was not in any way or form interested in him.

I didn't want to be stuck in an awkward position since I would be working on his team indefinitely, so I went to my own direct manager to tell her what happened and how I felt uncomfortable working directly with that client executive. As it turned out, she wasn't surprised at all. She got extremely annoyed with the situation and complained to me that this wasn't the first time this has happened with this particular client executive and other female consultants on the team. She assured me she wasn't going to allow him to make me feel uncomfortable. Moving forward, she asked me to copy her on any communications that I had with him, and if for whatever reason I had to meet with him, I should invite her to the meeting as well. She also told me she was going to have a word with him, and while I'm not sure what transpired in their meeting, my interactions with the client executive going forward were strictly business. A couple months later, I found out we would no longer be working with him, and I'd heard through the office rumor mill that a harassment complaint had been filed against him.

In another instance, I was working on a different project that required me to go on client site visits, which involved riding in a truck with a technician all day to observe and document their processes so that I could make process and technology improvement recommendations and help plan out strategies for our client. It meant visiting the truck depots and getting paired with one of hundreds of technicians going out that day. Technicians at the truck depot were made up of company employees and contractors. However, at the time I was doing the site visits, they were mostly contractors. The biggest difference between the company employees and contract technicians was the training they received. Company employees were trained not just on how to do their jobs but also on best practices as well as behavioral and compliance training, while the contract technicians just needed to know how to do their jobs.

On my site visits, I would go with the technicians as they did their service installations and repairs. Sometimes we were met by extremely angry customers who were upset because their service was not working. Other times, we were met with unfriendly pets (there was one time I found myself hightailing it back to the truck!), but it was all in a day's work.

Most of the time the site visits were uneventful; the technician was nice or indifferent to me being there and it was business as usual. However, there were many times where it was just unpleasant, and I had to ride in a truck all day with a contractor technician who would not behave professionally. There would be uncomfortable questions and catcalls. Or they would be extremely rude and dismissive. There was even a day when one technician decided to make inappropriate jokes about me at every customer home we visited. There were many times I had to warn a technician to be professional or ask him not to talk to me in a certain way, and I made complaints to the technician managers at the truck depot about their technicians' behaviors. I had been warned about this behavior by the other female consultants on my team who also had to go on site visits. In fact, most of the conversations we had about our experiences were full of complaints, but we just went along with it. We knew the site visits assignment would only last a couple months and then we wouldn't have to deal with it again.

However, after too many instances of unpleasant site visits, I started dreading going to work. I didn't want to go to the truck depot, having no idea what kind of person I would be stuck with for the day. So I talked to my manager about what I'd been experiencing on some of the site visits and to see if I could be assigned to employee technicians instead of contractors, since those were the technicians I was typically having issues with.

Instead of trying to understand what was happening, my manager said that myself and the rest of the other female consultants complained too much and we just needed to stick it out and do what we were paid to do because we needed to get the client's work done. She then went on to tell me that I should stop wearing makeup, pull my hair back, wear pants, and find some ugly shoes. And with that, the conversation was over.

I left the meeting feeling bad that I had even complained. Maybe I just needed to stick with it, like my manager had said. After all, it was only for a couple more months. I could put up with some unruly technicians for a short period of time, right? But the more I thought about it, the more I disagreed with her approach. Why shouldn't I be able to wear makeup to work? Why should I have to pull my hair back? I never dressed inappropriately at work when I wore my dresses or skirts and what if I didn't want to wear pants. . .or ugly shoes? Why would she give me that kind of advice?

When I got home, I called up a female senior consultant whom I had worked with on a previous project and had become friends with. I told her what was happening. She said, *"Sure, you can put up with some unruly technicians, but why should you have to? Your manager should be making sure you feel safe at work. She should be talking to the clients about best practices for their contractor technicians on the site visits."* I completely agreed with her. So, the next day, I went back to my senior manager, and instead of trying to explain my experience to her, I simply told her I did not feel comfortable going on site visits for the reasons I had stated the previous day. She couldn't force me to do it, but she was annoyed and had to adjust the schedule accordingly.

Once word got around that I wasn't going, none of the other female consultants on my team wanted to go on the site visits, either. It took a while, but HR training was provided to the contractor technicians after several complaints went above my manager. I was disappointed that she had responded the way she had. But the experience was another reminder that when it came to the real world, I had to learn how to advocate for and protect myself.

Despite the sometimes-difficult work environment, I continued to work above and beyond expectations. And I eventually got promoted. The work was challenging, but a lot of times it was fun. However, I was starting to crave a less hectic pace of life. In the consulting world, the client always came first—many times at expense of your personal life. I worked with other women who traveled so much that they rarely got to see their partners, children, or other family and friends. The hours were long and tedious, and there was always a pressing deliverable or client emergency. I remember being asked to be "available" on weekends and even on vacation. I always felt obligated to check emails when I wasn't working so I wouldn't fall behind on my work deliverables. It was hard to maintain any balance, and combined with the side hustles I was brewing here and there, it was just really difficult.

Around this time, my interest in the personal finance world had grown beyond more than just a simple interest. I had signed up for my employer's retirement savings plan and was teaching myself to invest when I fell into the world of personal finance bloggers. These were people who were paying off debt, saving for specific goals, and pursuing early retirement. These people were going against the status-quo and setting themselves up intentionally to live their best lives. They were traveling, starting businesses, paying off mortgages, and so much more. I remember reading blogs like "And Then She Saved" and "Get Rich Slowly," and before I knew it, I had a bookmarks folder on my computer full of personal finance blogs I would visit every day. I got so inspired that I decided to start my own personal blog on the then-popular platform Blogger.com, where I wrote about my life and my finances. It was called Lookbook by Onada (Onada is my middle name) and then later, Onada's Musings. Little did I know that I was setting the stage for what I do today, but at the time, the idea for Clever Girl Finance was still several years away.

From following these bloggers, I became extremely motivated to create a financial plan that would allow me to be independent of any employer and would give me the freedom to make my own personal choices independent of a paycheck. I was all in. I delved deeper into saving and investing and I started chronicling it all on my personal blog. I also started thinking about ways to further increase my income. After trying out a few different things, I stumbled into wedding and lifestyle photography, which, when I think back on it, really happened by chance.

A friend of mine was getting married in Jamaica, and since I'd never been to the Caribbean, I thought it would be a good idea to buy a good camera to document my first trip. I dipped into my savings and purchased an entry-level professional

Nikon camera. It was amazing compared to the little point-and-shoot I previously owned.

Growing up, my dad had several professional cameras and was always taking photos of me and my brothers. (We have boxes and boxes of photos filled with the best memories from our childhoods.) As a result of my dad's interest in photography, I developed my own and always wanted to have a good camera. My trip to Jamaica was the perfect time to buy one.

In Jamaica, I was the girl with the camera around her neck the entire trip. I took pictures of everything. My friend, who was getting married, noticed. On the day of her wedding, for whatever reasons, her wedding photographer was running late, so she asked me to take some photos of her getting ready. I was nervous because I didn't want to mess up her photos, but I happily accepted. When I got back from the trip, I got a free trial of some editing software online and taught myself how to do basic photo touch-ups with various tutorials I found. It took me hours to get it done, and when I gave her the photo files from her wedding, she was extremely happy. That was when I realized that maybe I was onto something.

So, I put an ad on Craigslist offering to photograph a wedding for free. (This was before Facebook was what it is today and Instagram did not yet exist.) I wanted to see what it would be like to photograph a wedding, and if I would like it. By offering my services for free, there was less pressure for me if the photos didn't turn out great. I didn't really expect anyone to take me seriously. I mean, who would trust a photographer with no experience to take pictures of one of the most important days of their lives?! But one couple did. They were getting married on a really tight budget and loved the sound of free photos, so they reached out to me.

Their wedding day arrived and I had an incredible time taking their photos. I'd found a "suggested wedding shots" list on a photography forum and used that as my guide for the pictures I absolutely needed to get. The bride and groom were very hands off and not the least bit worried that I might not know what I was doing. I, on the other hand, focused on overcompensating for my lack of photography skills by taking as many photos as I possibly could so I could increase my odds of culling a good set of photos for the couple. After the wedding, I organized the photos and started to edit them each night after work based on what I'd learned from editing my friend's photos from Jamaica. A couple of weeks later, I delivered the images to the couple.

They were ecstatic. So ecstatic that they even gave me a $300 tip, which I absolutely did not expect. And so, with my new confidence as a photographer, I put out additional ads for weddings, engagement sessions, and lifestyle sessions, and photography became my main side hustle. I bought books, joined photography forums, went to meetups, and practiced on my friends and family. It wasn't long before I built up a solid portfolio and the brides whose weddings I'd photographed started sharing my services with other brides-to-be that they knew. Through that word of mouth, my photography business started to grow. As a result, I was able to raise my prices, charging $3,500 to $5,000 per wedding, depending on what was involved and how long I'd be there. In turn, I invested in my side hustle, bought better gear and software, and saved and invested the rest of the money I made after taxes.

Working full time and running this busy side hustle became a real balancing act. I worked at my consulting job 50+ hours a week, then spent early mornings and nights during the week editing photos (many times in a hotel room because I was on a work trip). On most weekends, I had sessions or events to photograph, usually on Friday nights, all day on Saturdays, and all day on Sundays. I was exhausted, but I loved it.

About five years into it, the stressful pace of my consulting job and the constant travel, combined with my busy photography side hustle, began to wear on me. Fortunately, things were about to change. I had just wrapped up a big project where my client was so impressed by my performance that they offered me a job at their company. This meant leaving my consulting employer to go work for my client full-time. I decided it would be a good opportunity to slow down a bit and catch my breath. And so, I negotiated an exit plan with my employer so I could go work for the client full-time. I negotiated everything I could possibly negotiate before taking on the new position.

Even though I had already worked with this client before, I was an employee instead of a consultant, which meant my work life changed dramatically. As an employee, my projects and deliverables had less stringent timelines, and most people worked a strict nine-to-five. I quickly came to realize this was because all of the expectations to get stuff done, especially on high-priority projects, was placed on the consultants. There I was getting paid more money with a lot less stress, which meant more time to focus on my side hustle. I should have made the move sooner!

I spent the next few years growing my photography business. I established a stronger portfolio, built a website, and over time brides began to find me not only through word of mouth but also through online searches. As my clientele grew, I continued to raise my prices and charge more money. I got to the point where my photography side hustle became a major source of supplemental income, which really helped me accelerate achieving some of the financial goals I had set for myself. During this time, I also switched jobs two more times (always for more money, better positions, and better opportunities). I even had younger mentees at work who came to me for advice. I ultimately got to a point where I loved what I did for work and for my side hustle.

As I reflect on my career, I would describe the 11 years I worked full time as the defining years in my life, especially when it came to really getting comfortable with negotiating, speaking up, and advocating for myself. When I started my very first job, I certainly didn't think I was stepping into my "career-defining years." As a matter of fact, in the early days of my career, I was simply going through the motions of getting up day after day and going to work to earn a paycheck. It even got mundane. Weeks would pass where I'd have done the same thing over and over again a hundred times; I'd wake up, get ready, go to work, do work, come home, and rinse and repeat the next day, without giving it much thought.

But discovering that I was the lowest earner in my work peer group was the catalyst for me to become more intentional about my career. This was the beginning of me building my career confidence, making sure my work was recognized, not allowing myself to be taken advantage of based on my gender, and essentially making the most of what I was working with.

My career experiences and everything I learned along the way gave me the opportunity to leverage the exchange I was making; I was exchanging my time for income, but also exchanging my time for important experiences and lessons that would help me grow in so many ways beyond the biweekly paycheck I was earning to pay my bills. Yes, I went to work every day, giving up my time to earn money. But every project I worked on, every professional relationship I built, every mistake I made, and even every difficult encounter I faced at work all contributed to my personal, emotional, and mental growth. And as I learned about financial wellness along the way, every check I earned from my full-time job and my side hustle allowed me to contribute toward the financial goals I'd set for my future self. All of these experiences were preparing me for the phase of my life that would come next—the phase that includes Clever Girl Finance.

So, let me ask you this: Is there a catalyst on your career path that you have yet to recognize? Do you feel like you need to be more intentional about your career goals? I would challenge you to seek out these catalysts, reflect on them, and take action on any potential opportunities to advocate for yourself and your success. As women, advocating for ourselves (and for each other) is incredibly important, especially given the challenges around pay and gender equality. Even if you own your own business, it is still incredibly important for you. Every time you stand up and advocate for yourself, you not only help yourself but you could also be empowering another woman coming up behind you who is facing the same challenges. You can lead by example and be the motivation or role model she needs. You can drive changes to rules and policies that are not favorable for women in the workplace or in the business world.

Don't be afraid to be bold on your career path. It might take practice as you step into your own, but remember your self-worth and the immense value you bring to your employers. It was not always easy for me to have difficult conversations or take hard actions. But I had to tell myself that I was worth the higher negotiation, I was worth the change I was pushing for, and I owed it to myself to want to do better and be better. Each time I did it, I was choosing to prosper in my career versus simply sitting back and accepting what was handed to me.

WHAT I'VE LEARNED

When I started working in corporate America, I simply settled for whatever I was given. But in those early days of my career journey, I learned that if I was going to be successful at work, especially as a woman, I needed to take control of my own trajectory. Taking control meant asking for what I deserved to be paid, learning how to negotiate beyond just my income, and becoming confident enough to call out instances of inappropriateness. I also learned that I could still follow my passions and create additional income opportunities through my side hustles while still being successful at work. It took stepping out of my comfort zone and developing my self-confidence to take the control I needed. In retrospect, it was necessary; otherwise I would have done myself a great disservice.

LET'S TALK ABOUT YOU

The early years of your career can be some of the most defining years of your life, and even if you are beyond those early years, looking back on them can be extremely insightful. It's important to take advantage of and reflect on every opportunity that comes your way that could help you succeed or drive change. Here are some questions to help you reflect on your career so far:

- Is there a catalyst on your career path that you have yet to recognize? For me, it was finding out that most of my peers had negotiated higher salaries. What's it for you?
- Do you feel like you need to be more intentional about your career goals?
- Are there opportunities in your workplace that are staring right at you that you might be ignoring or have yet to take advantage of?
- Are you negotiating for what you're worth?
- Are you calling out inappropriateness and indiscretions?

Reflect on these questions and lay out your answers to help you identify the steps you need to take to advocate for and prioritize yourself. It could be getting really clear about the career goals you need to take action on, finding and speaking with a mentor, getting comfortable with negotiating your next raise, salary, or business contract, introducing a new source of income, having difficult conversations, or calling out inappropriate behavior.

By being intentional and taking action, it will get easier and easier to take advantage of opportunities when they arise, even when fear rears its ugly head. When fear seems like it's taking over, remind yourself of your value and why you are worth it.

CHAPTER 4

Changing Paths to Financial Wellness

You might not be certain that the next path is the right one, but you owe it to yourself to do your best, regardless. So, trust your intuition but be strategic.

As I was building my career, life was also happening outside of work. My boyfriend of five years had proposed and we had begun planning our wedding. At the time, I was working and living in New Jersey, but getting married meant I'd be moving to Philadelphia, where he was completing his professional training. Then, a year later, we'd be moving to New York City for a specialty program he wanted to pursue. Fortunately, my employer had their headquarters in Philadelphia and so I was able to transfer to a position there not long after we moved. Philly had become home. It's where my mom lived when I first moved to the States, and it's where I stayed when I took my one year off from college. I had gotten to know the city really well.

We spent the first few months after our move getting ready for our traditional Yoruba wedding, which we traveled to Nigeria for. I'd met my boyfriend in high school in Nigeria and we'd reconnected years later in New York City. We chose to have our traditional wedding in Nigeria since the bulk of our extended families lived there. The traditional wedding was in honor of our cultural roots and what traditional marriage represents in our culture—the joining of not just a couple but two families. It involved an elaborate ceremony moderated by representatives of both families and over-the-top gifts that my fiancé's family presented to my parents and family elders.

I like to say our traditional wedding was really for our parents, especially since the actual wedding ceremony was about three hours long and mostly involved them. I only participated in the last 30 or so minutes of it, prior to which I spent the entire time waiting to be announced in a separate room while my friends kept me company. My husband, however, got to participate in more of the ceremony, since he had to go through a series of family greetings and then wait for me to be presented to him.

A few months after our traditional wedding, it was time for our Christian wedding. Having two weddings is not uncommon across Nigerian cultures. The traditional wedding is more for the parents and extended family, while the Christian wedding is more for the couple. Our Christian wedding took place in Philadelphia, and we invited our close friends and family members who lived stateside. It was a short ceremony at an Episcopal church (which is a subset of the Anglican faith we were both raised with) and a big reception afterward. Both of our weddings were incredible experiences, and I have beautiful and vivid memories that will stay with me forever.

As a result of all the wedding planning, the year went by pretty quickly, and soon it was time to start thinking about our move to New York City. We still had about seven months to go before we had to move, but I was anxious to find a job as soon as possible. With two weddings under our belts, we'd spent a lot of money, and I didn't want to have a break in my income that would cause us to spend even more of our savings. We wanted to get back to focusing on our financial goals now that the weddings were over.

At this early state of our marriage, I was the breadwinner since my husband was still training for his career, so I started my job hunt early. I contacted people in my network from my consulting days, and within a month I had interviewed and landed a new and better-paying job in New York City, this time working as a business analyst. I actually expected the job hunt to take me a few months, so I was surprised when I landed one a month after I began my search. I accepted the new position immediately because I didn't want to miss out on the opportunity. The challenge, however, was that I lived in Philadelphia and my new job was all the way on the west side of Manhattan in New York City (about two and a half hours one way, door to door). Of course, I told my new employer nothing about this. All they needed to know was that I would be there on time every day. I didn't want give them any reasons whatsoever not to hire me.

So, I quickly went about exploring my options. Driving five hours a day would take too much of a toll on me (and my car), and that was assuming there wouldn't be any traffic. If you know how commuting into New York City works during rush hour, you know this assumption was totally wrong; there's always traffic. My next option was public transportation. I found out that the Greyhound bus had a commuter line from New Jersey into Manhattan with priority lane access, which minimized how much traffic I'd be stuck in. But it meant that I'd have to drive 25 minutes from Philadelphia to the bus stop in New Jersey, get on the bus for 1 hour and 45 minutes to the Port Authority Bus Terminal in Manhattan, and then hop on the subway for a few stops before I would arrive at work. Door to door, including waiting time, would take me about three hours each way. That was six hours of commuting every single weekday. Just thinking about it now is exhausting and I'm not sure how I did it, but I did it for six entire months before we moved to New York City.

My days were incredibly long. I would wake up at 4 a.m. to be at work by 8 a.m., and I wouldn't get home until after 9 p.m.

At work, even though I talked about myself with my boss, I never really shared "where" I lived until he asked me one day, a month into my new job. At that time, our office had a strict "no work from home" policy, but after finding out about my commute, he allowed me to work from home on Fridays if there were no major meetings. The arrangement was just between us; HR would not have approved it. This was a huge saving grace because I got to work from home two to three times a month. On my commute, I would sleep (a lot), read books, watch Netflix on my phone, or catch up on work on my laptop. I kept up with delivering my best work, and while it was painful, those six months flew by. Once we moved to New York, my commute went from six hours a day to a 20-minute walk each way. It was such a relief to be able to sleep in.

I worked at that job as a business analyst for four years, and by this time, we'd moved to a different part of New Jersey and my husband and I started thinking about having kids. We'd initially chosen to wait to have kids since we were moving so much, but now that he was done with his training and I was settled into my career, it made sense. Over the next 18 months or so I got pregnant and gave birth to healthy, almost full-term twin babies after an incredibly difficult pregnancy and five months of strict bedrest. I didn't know it at the time, but giving birth to my babies was the beginning of an inflection point in my career.

I'll be completely honest and say as a new mom I struggled. Managing two newborns who slept very little (even with help) was hard, especially in the early days. My husband went back to work after a week of paternity leave and the first nanny I hired to help me quit after two days because, in her words, *"Twins were just so much more work than I expected."* I was also dealing with postpartum depression, which I didn't actually recognize until I reflected back on it a couple years later. I felt isolated and exhausted. I loved my babies beyond words, but I also started feeling like I had lost myself. People mostly asked about my twins and not about me. My life had changed so dramatically with two new precious lives to take care of, and it took me a while to get adjusted to my new life as a mom. I definitely have a special sense of compassion for new and first-time moms after my own personal experience.

In addition, I was dreading going back to work, even though my return was still weeks away. Sure, I loved my job. But my whole perspective about the work I was doing had changed in terms of how meaningful it was, especially now that I had a truly meaningful job as a new mom. Just as I was about to head back to work, I found a great nanny and my mom and my aunt made themselves available to me to help out as much as they could that first year. However, that nagging question of *"How truly meaningful is my work?"* didn't go away. I began toying with the idea of starting another business as an alternative to my full-time job, but I had absolutely no idea what I wanted to do. Every time I would try to come up with a new idea, I would draw blanks. My photography business was still there, but I had taken some time off from it during my pregnancy and for the first several months after I gave birth. And so, I started writing down random ideas of things I enjoyed doing and topics I was interested in. I had actually started doing this while I was pregnant, but now I was more intentional about it because of how I was feeling. I did this over the next year, but nothing in particular spoke to me and so I just kept at it with work.

I changed jobs once more during this time when my company got acquired. It was a good opportunity for me to find a job with a shorter commute home, since I was now living in New Jersey but still commuting to New York City. All the while I continued to write down any ideas that came to me. I wrote down all sorts of things, and after a while I started to notice a pattern; every one of the ideas I wrote down— whether it was in fashion, retail, motherhood, photography, or technology—were in one way or the other related to affordability, budgeting, and financial wellness. Maybe I could package all of my ideas into one place and make it an interesting resource for women? I wasn't sure yet.

One day, a friend of mine was visiting from out of town because she wanted to meet my twins, who were now 13 months old. While they napped, we began talking about our careers, job fulfillment, and business. I vividly remember telling her about my brainstorming process over the last year and about this idea I had to put all my interests together and create a site for women. I was explaining to her how I wasn't sure about my idea yet when she interrupted me and said, *"You should totally to do it. This is everything you talk about all the time!"* Well, she wasn't lying. I certainly found a way to talk about money with my friends all the time. Whether it was about my side hustles, how I was saving and investing, or my future financial goals, I always had something to say about money. I did this on my earlier mentioned personal blog (Lookbook by Onada), that went on to gain some traction. I talked about saving to splurge, my money mistakes, my investing approach, fashion and style, my newest purchases, and more. Sometimes I would run a savings challenge for a few weeks and ask the women who read my blog to comment on how much money they were saving each week. I even created an entire financial planning journal in a Word document once and emailed it to all my friends for their feedback.

In that moment when my friend made that comment, I realized what I needed all this while was some signal that my idea made sense—and her comment was the signal I needed. I also realized that the reason the signal had evaded me was because I hadn't talked about my idea out loud at all. I hadn't even mentioned it to my husband, because I just wasn't sure what it was. But now, my idea was starting to make sense. I shared it with my husband and my other close friends, and they were excited. A few years later, the friend whom I had first shared the idea with would remind me of that moment, *"Can you believe this all started with you saying, I have this idea...?!"*

As that was happening, I was also coming to the realization that I was reliving my mother's experiences that I had observed as a young child. She was raising young children and trying to stand on her own feet financially. She had seen friends unable to leave difficult relationships, excluded from their household financial planning and even navigating divorces with very few financial options in the aftermath. I was now going through my own big transitions in life and so were many of my female friends. However, there weren't a lot of physical or online resources available as it related to personal finance specifically *for* women *by* women. To me, this was a very important gap that needed to be filled, especially when it came to truly understanding the life transitions and emotions women face when it comes to money. My friends were switching careers, navigating relationships, getting married, and/or having babies. Some were getting divorced, dealing with losses, or trying to find their footing at work or with life in general. In every single scenario, money was a concern, even if it was just in the background. And for a lot of friends and even colleagues at work, talking about money was confusing, embarrassing, or something they just didn't want to deal with. This was the second signal that my idea made sense.

The truth was (and still is) that most people weren't raised talking about saving and investing around the dinner table. As women, we typically weren't raised to talk about money at all, and this transcends generationally because neither were most of our mothers or grandmothers. In society, especially in prior generations, being vocal about or overly involved in finances simply was not a woman's place. In fact, until the Equal Credit Opportunity Act[1] was signed into law in 1974, women were limited financially by society itself. A woman could not apply for a mortgage, take out a line of credit, or even open a bank account without her husband's permission. And if she was single, then she was completely shut out without a male co-signer. While this type of discrimination is no longer legal, the prejudices still remain.

I remember that a few years after graduating college I had saved a significant amount of money and decided to visit a financial planner for some guidance. Before even taking the time to understand my financial goals and why I was there, he immediately assumed that I had been given the money by a rich boyfriend or husband and was surprised to learn

---

[1]The US Department of Justice, The Equal Credit Opportunity Act, updated September 24, 2021, https://www.justice.gov/crt/equal-credit-opportunity-act-3

I had earned it all on my own as a single woman. More recently, a friend of mine visited another financial planner to get guidance on paying off her large student loans, and his immediate response to her inquiry was, *"Your best option is to marry rich; it's easier."* He may have thought he was making a funny joke, but she didn't find it funny in the least bit. These examples aren't to give financial planners a bad rap. These were just two planners in a sea of many incredibly talented professionals in the industry. However, it does illustrate that the perception of a woman's "supposed" place is still held by many in today's society.

Looking back at prior generations, if a woman was able to create financial success for herself, in many instances all kinds of excuses were made as to why she was successful, implying her success was a crux:

> *Oh, that's why she's single.*
> *Oh, that's why she's divorced.*
> *Oh, that's why she doesn't have kids.*
> *Oh, that's why. . . .*
> *She's too money minded.*
> *She's too business focused.*

The sad part is that these types of judgmental excuses are still made today about successful women. I've even had to deal with this judgment personally (which I'll talk more about in the next chapter). But knowing what I know from my own mother and observing and learning from the other women in my family, prioritizing financial wellness as a woman is incredibly important, especially in the world we live in today where the tables are turning so quickly.

While we absolutely cannot ignore the impact of the gender wage gap on our earning capabilities, compared to our mother's and grandmother's generation, we are earning more money on average than they did. Plus, so many women in today's world are choosing not to get married, are happily becoming breadwinners in their families, and are taking the world by storm as single mothers and sole providers. Add on the statistic that women are living longer on average than men[2] and will need more money to sustain themselves in retirement as a result, and it's easy to see why financial wellness for women is more important than ever. All of this led to the beginning of my mission with Clever Girl Finance.

It did, however, take me a few months to make it "official." Once my idea was firmly set in my mind, I got to work on having a website built and I started writing articles and creating other content. I even invested $6,000 in startup costs in preparation to launch. Everything was on track and ready to go, but I stalled my launch at the last second. In all honesty, I was afraid of putting my idea out into the world, and I wasn't sure how it would be received, even though I had been blogging and talking about money for years. I had been updating one of my friends as I was preparing for my launch, and she was just as passionate about my mission as I was. She would call or text me every few days to ask when I was launching the website and to remind me how much women needed the information I had to share. Needless to say, she was floored when she found out I'd stalled the launch. We eventually agreed that I would launch the website on her

---

[2]https://www.cdc.gov/nchs/data/factsheets/factsheet_nvss.pdf

birthday or I would owe her money—a lot of money. That was enough motivation, along with the $6,000 I'd already invested, to put the very first iteration of Clever Girl Finance out into the world on August 10, 2015.

Initially, I was able to balance working full-time while I ran my photography business and Clever Girl Finance as side hustles. I was exhausted from work and photography, but Clever Girl Finance was so exciting. I was building a brand-new business that I was extremely passionate about, and I was learning so much along the way. The focus was financial wellness, but behind the scenes I was learning about content creation, social media marketing, email marketing, and having tons and tons of conversations with women who fit into my ideal avatar to learn what their specific financial concerns and struggles were.

My schedule was as follows: I would wake up every weekday around 4:30 a.m. to work on my businesses for a couple of hours. Then around 6:30 a.m., I'd wake up my twins to get them ready for daycare, drop them off, and head to work to be there by 8:30 a.m. Over lunch, I'd eat at my desk and work on my businesses and then leave to pick up my kids at 5:30 p.m. We'd get home, I'd make dinner, get my kids ready for bed, and then stay up a couple more hours until about 11 or midnight, again working on my businesses. On the weekends, I was up early as well, and all my spare time outside of time with my husband and kids went into running my photography business and building Clever Girl Finance. Although I made the effort to keep in touch, my schedule meant spending less time with friends and extended family.

As Clever Girl Finance started to gain traction, I decided to completely transition away from my photography business so I could better manage my time. My photography business required me to be away from home for extended periods of time and then spend hours editing photos after work. This was taking a toll on my family life, especially with two active toddlers. And in all honesty, my passion had shifted to growing Clever Girl Finance.

However, that transition alone wasn't enough. Eventually, I got to a point where something else had to give. I realized that if I wanted to really grow Clever Girl Finance, I needed to spend more time dedicated to building it. The early mornings and late nights just weren't cutting it anymore. I had so much to do for both my full-time job and Clever Girl Finance, in addition to caring for my family, that I was deliriously tired. And as a result, I found myself making mistakes at work and in my business. I'd tried to make it all work for a long time, but I really needed to decide how to move forward, because it was obvious that my current approach was no longer sustainable.

That said, it absolutely didn't make any sense to just up and quit my job without a plan, because at the time, even though Clever Girl Finance was growing, it was barely making any money. But I believed so much in my business and that it was part of my purpose that I decided to take a chance: I'd work on Clever Girl Finance full time for 12 months to see if I could make any progress on it. And if not, I'd go back to work full time.

In order to take this chance, I wanted to make sure I had money in the bank to act as a buffer. This meant that instead of quitting my job right away, I set a goal to save 12–18 months of money to cover the cost of my household financial obligations. By doing this, I could fully focus on my business without placing any financial stress on myself or my husband and without having to tap into our savings. I know so many people who have started businesses and cashed out their savings and 401(k) accounts, but that type of risk was not one I was willing to take. My savings goals and long-term plans needed to stay intact. So, I focused on saving my buffer, and two years after I started Clever Girl Finance, I was able to quit my job to run my business full time.

The moment I gave my boss my resignation notice, I felt a massive sense of regret and irresponsibility. Was I really going to give up my comfortable six-figure income, my 401(k) match, and my future bonuses to run a business that wasn't yet making any money? It seemed crazy to me. I wanted to go back to my boss and tell him I'd changed my mind (he was already making me all kinds of offers so I wouldn't quit). But my gut told me I was doing the right thing. Plus, I had the encouragement of my parents, my husband, and the few friends I'd shared the idea with, so I stood by my decision.

Months after I quit, and even as I started to make slow but steady progress in building Clever Girl Finance, I still kept my cover letter and resume up to date and would apply for jobs here and there. I even went on a few job interviews and got a job offer, which I declined. I was all about keeping my options open, just in case things didn't work out. Those months after leaving my job, I worked my butt off and the hours I freed up after leaving my full-time job were quickly taken over by Clever Girl Finance work, but it was worth it.

Within 18 months, the business had grown further, and while still small, it began to earn steady revenue that allowed me to pay myself a small salary.

I took a leap of faith, trusted my intuition, and I did it. I created a fallback plan just in case things didn't work out. But most importantly, I was taking my first step toward doing work that I was passionate about and that was truly meaningful to me. Not only that, the work I was doing was positively impacting the lives of the women my business reached, and I was a building a legacy for children. This was how Clever Girl Finance got started, and I truly believe that if I hadn't trusted my gut and taken that leap of faith, I would have massive regrets about it today.

Sometimes the next path you need to take is not always apparent to you. And many times, once you determine what that next path is, you're not certain if it's the right one to take. After all the hard work it's taken to get to a certain point, the last thing you want to feel is like you're making a big mistake that could jeopardize all of that hard work. That's definitely how I felt when I quit my job to run my business full time and stood staring down the path of the unknown. However, the truth is, if you don't try, you'll never know. And in my case, I certainly didn't want to feel regret about what could've been if only I had tried.

Maybe you're at a similar inflection point in your career, your relationship, or in another area of your life, and you need to make a big decision and chose a path that could potentially get you closer to a big dream or a greater purpose. Taking a leap of faith can be scary and nerve-racking. But my advice to you is this: you owe it to yourself to do your best, so trust your intuition but be strategic. Determine what your options are, give yourself a timeline, and create a fallback plan. This will give you the confidence to know that whatever the outcome, you have a plan to keep moving forward, no matter what.

WHAT I'VE LEARNED

At one point or the other, we all experience a stage (or stages) in our lives where we don't know if we are making the right decisions but we trust our gut feeling and make the decisions anyway. This is what I did when I decided to make that crazy commute to and from New York City and when I later decided to start yet another side hustle on top of my full-time job despite my challenges as a new mom. Each decision was scary and nerve-racking and I would think about everything that could possibly go wrong, but I realized that thinking that way would keep me dead in my tracks. And so, I learned to shift my mindset to focus less on the cons and more on the pros of the decisions I needed to make. I also learned that not every choice I made needed to have a defined outcome, as long as I was willing to make things work the best way I could and readjust as necessary. And so that's what I did.

LET'S TALK ABOUT YOU

Taking a leap of faith can be scary and nerve-racking. But you can approach it intentionally, which will in turn help you make the best objective decisions to move forward. Here are some questions to help you think things through:

- What opportunities or chances is your intuition telling you to take?

- What fears are holding you back from chasing those opportunities?

- What are the pros and cons of each opportunity or chance?

- How would they radically change your life if you pursued them?

- What buffer or fallback plans can you put in place so you're better prepared to take the next steps?

Now is a great time to commit to believing in yourself. Make the decision that you will take advantage of the opportunities that will come your way. You may not be able to predict the outcome, but sometimes it's necessary to simply trust the process and take the leap.

CHAPTER 5

My $100k Savings Story

People may not always like what you have to say, but stand in your truth and remember your why.

One of the first major pivotal growth points for Clever Girl Finance was as a result of me sharing my personal savings story of how I saved $100,000 in a little over three years right after college as a single woman. While I've reached many milestones in my personal finances, this was my first major milestone and a story I chose to share publicly after a lot of deliberation.

I was about a year into the business and at this point was sharing weekly success stories on the Clever Girl Finance blog and Instagram account from different women about how they'd saved money, paid off debt, or overcome financial obstacles as part of our inspiration series. I wanted to showcase the success stories, including stories in progress, from different women who came from all walks of life as a way to inspire our audience regardless of where they were in their financial journey. One day I was going through the comments when I noticed someone said, *"Bola, I'd love to read your own story about how you've achieved your financial goals."* And so, I thought to myself, maybe I should share how I crossed my first $100,000 savings milestone. However, being the introverted person that I am, I was extremely hesitant and, to be honest, even afraid.

To me, this was very different from sharing my savings story on my lifestyle blog in my little old corner of the internet. It felt more public and more personal. I was worried that it might come across as me showing off or trying to brag. I really had to think hard about it. As usual, I leaned on my support team and spoke to my husband and close friends about this idea. They thought it made perfect sense to share it and reminded me of the "why" behind starting Clever Girl

Finance. Plus, I was already sharing amazing stories from other women; why wasn't my own story part of the mix? I had gained so much personally from hearing the stories of other women. Plus, I knew I could use my own story to motivate and inspire others to succeed, especially at a time when resources for women (especially black and brown women) were few and far between.

I thought back to an experience when I was at the beginning of my savings journey, where I had walked into a bookstore hoping to find a personal finance book for women. I wanted a book specifically for women and written by a woman that was focused on my particular needs and concerns as one. As I browsed the personal finance book section at that bookstore, I found books on retirement planning, wills and trusts, real estate investing, stock market trading, general personal finance, and a single book on personal finance for women. It was a *New York Times* bestseller on this particular topic, but ironically enough, it was written by a man. While I bought that book and loved it (I read it to shreds), I'd always wished it had been written by a woman sharing her own perspective and not by a man sharing the perspective of a woman in his life. As I continued on my financial journey, I would later find three other personal finance books for women (this time written by women). But in the vast sea of personal finance books written from a male perspective, these books were hardly enough. We needed more resources and more relatable stories that were for and by women.

And so, after much deliberation, I built up the courage and decided to share my savings story. I believed that having gone through the experience myself, saving a large amount of money was attainable for other people. More importantly, I had to remind myself that starting Clever Girl Finance and now sharing my personal story was not about me "showing off." It was instead about me adding my voice and experiences to the multitude of stories I was sharing through the brand's platform to provide yet another perspective to showcase that there wasn't just one way to achieve financial wellness—there were several. By having this variety of perspectives, any woman reading these stories—regardless of her background or upbringing—could find one that she saw herself in and that she could relate to. This was the goal.

The first time I shared my story on the Clever Girl Finance blog, I laid out everything I did to save that $100,000 after graduating college, starting with the salary from my very first corporate job where I earned $54,000 before taxes. I was honest about the advantages I had, which included not having any student loans, thanks to the sacrifices of my incredible mother, being fortunate enough to get employed almost immediately after graduation, and the fact that I was able to increase my salary over that three-and-half-year period through raises, bonuses, and promotions, which raised my salary to around $74,000 by the time I reached my savings milestone. I also had a lucrative side hustle (my photography business) that earned me money on top of my salary and allowed me to really accelerate my savings.

I talked about how I contributed to my 401(k) plan, taking advantage of the free money (aka employer's contribution match) that was made available to me. At the time, my employer matched 100 percent of the first 6 percent that I contributed. I didn't max out my contributions right away, but I did contribute around 15 percent of my salary. And throughout the three-and-half years I worked there, I was able to save about $40,000 alone in my retirement account.

I talked about how I focused on keeping my expenses low even though I had a car note, insurance, and a mortgage that I was paying on my first condo. (I did, however, live at home with my mom the first six months after graduation before I moved into my condo, and this definitely helped to kickstart my savings journey.) My groceries were never a big deal, as I was single and worked so much that I barely had time to cook. My staple meal was ramen noodles, which, while not particularly healthy or nutritious, was extremely cheap.

I was also the girl who would walk around the office to see if there was a baby shower, retirement party, or senior executive meeting going on that might have leftover breakfast or lunch. I did this so often that office assistants would let me know ahead of time when and where there was going to be free food. Going out was usually hanging out at friends' houses. And since I don't drink alcohol out of personal preference, I was able to save a lot of money there, too. My water bill, internet bill, and cell phone bill all came in at less than a couple hundred dollars combined each month.

By keeping my expenses low and being mindful of how I used credit, I was able to focus on saving 40 to 50 percent of my paychecks. I saved all of my yearly bonus, and I always saved the bulk of whatever tax return I got. As a result, I saved a ton of cash very quickly this way—about $18,000 a year on average. As the three years passed, I accumulated well over

$50,000 in cash savings from my full-time job. Combined with the earnings from my side hustle, I hit $100,000 in savings in just three-and-a-half years. And by the end of the fourth year of my savings journey, I had saved over $128,000.

My reason for saving this money was plain and simple. Knowing where I came from and the sacrifices that were made for me to be where I was, I felt obligated to do well and to make my family proud. Being irresponsible with the money I was fortunate enough to be earning was not an option. I could not let the sacrifices made for me be in vain. I had an opportunity, and I was going to take full advantage of it. That was it.

Generally, my saving story was well received. It quickly began to pick up traction from organic Google traffic, and much more so after I shared it on social media. Women were excited to read a financial success story from another woman, and I got emails and comments from strangers who told me that by reading my story they felt motivated or like they were on the right track. There were even women who emailed me to say they were proud of me for sharing my story because we needed more positive financial stories about women, especially women of color, out in the mainstream. I think the fact that this story was being shared by a woman—especially a black woman immigrant—made it even more interesting. I did several podcast interviews about my savings story, and it got picked up by other financial platforms. Before I knew it, I was getting visibility from larger media outlets, and in 2018, I even had a two-page spread in *Money* magazine that focused on my $100,000 savings achievement and shared my savings tips.

Of course, when you open yourself up to the public, there is bound to be criticism, and the trolls are never far behind. As my story gained more visibility in the proceeding years, there were those who thought my savings approach was completely unrealistic, especially when it came to cutting back on expenses or spending all those hours working on my side hustle trying to increase my income. There were also those who thought there was no way I could have ever saved that amount of money on my own. One female-focused platform referred to me as a "trust-fund baby" with a "working husband" on their social media account, implying that my story was a lie, even though they frequently repurposed Clever Girl Finance content on their website, including that specific savings story where my background and the fact that I was single were highlighted.

There was the interview for a self-help/motivational radio show where I was invited to share how I saved all that money in that amount of time. The show had hosts who asked me a series of questions so I could elaborate on my experience and give my personal tips and advice to their audience. The interview was going really well (or so I thought), until we hit commercial break. I guess the hosts forgot to mute themselves or didn't realize the mute was not on, because as the commercials played in the background, I could hear them talking. . .about me. The first host said, *"I call bullshit on this whole story. There's no way she saved $100,000 by herself."* The second host then responded, *"Right! I bet she had a rich boyfriend or a sponsor, you know these chicks never come clean."* I didn't interrupt them or chime in. I just listened to what they had to say. When we came back on air, it took my whole entire being and the grace of Jesus for me not to hang up on that radio interview. Instead, I focused on sharing my story and answering the questions their audience was calling in to ask and I completed the interview.

There were even people who went as far as sending me nasty messages via email and on social media to share their opinions about my story. I was told I was selfish for "putting my money in people's faces." I was told I should be "giving money to the less privileged instead of bragging about it online." Some people went as far as sending hateful racist and sexist messages about my appearance, including a profanity-filled message about how I didn't even look like I was worth a hundred dollars, much less a hundred thousand.

I'd be lying if I said those nasty comments didn't hurt, because they did. Especially those first few ones. They stung the worst, especially since sharing my story was done entirely with good intentions. However, over time, it got better. The nasty comments hurt less, and eventually, they rolled right off.

As I've navigated scenarios like these, I've continued to remind myself about the "why" behind sharing my story and starting my business, which is bigger than anyone's hateful opinion in the grand scheme of my goals and mission. I do, however, still find it baffling that the celebrities who spend frivolously and drop $100,000 on single shopping trips are widely celebrated for flossing. The guy who buys the latest luxury car or high-end five-figure designer watch is awed on social media. But when I shared how I saved money over years, some people still attempted to cloud my accomplishment with ridicule and judgment. Despite this, the positive impact of sharing my story far outweighed the negativity those certain people wanted to brew.

Sharing my story and gaining the interest of outlets in the personal finance space and mainstream media was and continues to be an amazing catalyst when it comes to brand awareness for Clever Girl Finance. It's led to so many incredible business opportunities and press as a result, including features on *Forbes*, *CNBC*, *Good Morning America*, *Fortune*, *Money*, *The Washington Post*, and many more.

The overwhelming majority of women who read my story and sent messages via email or social media said it inspired and motivated them and helped them create a plan for themselves. So many other women sent messages sharing their own success stories when it came to saving money or paying off debt. Their stories inspired many episodes of the Clever Girls Know podcast, which today is one of the top personal finance podcasts for women.

Through these experiences, I've learned that what's most important in life isn't what people have to say about me or even what they think about me. What's most important is that I honor myself by telling the truth, responding with grace, developing thick skin (especially as the face of my business), and reminding myself that what I have to offer, share, and give far outweighs any troll or hater, because at the end of the day, my goal is to pursue my purpose and have positive impact in everything I do.

In many instances, when you have a story to tell or something to share, it can be intimidating and nerve-racking. There's the fear of being judged or shamed. I've felt all of these feelings. Sometimes it's from strangers, and other times it's from the people closest to you (which can be incredibly disappointing).

But I encourage you to stand in your truth and pursue your why, regardless of what anyone has to say. They don't matter.

WHAT I'VE LEARNED

Being attacked about my savings accomplishment was an awful feeling. I questioned the point of sharing my story, I considered retreating, and I even told myself that I would never again share another personal success publicly. Thankfully, there was the support from my family, friends, and the incredible Clever Girl Finance community who reminded me of how my story was empowering others. This was the most important thing. I learned not everyone will cheer for me and not everyone wants to see me do well—and that's okay. I learned how to block the jabs and blows and keep my chin up because my mission is so much bigger than the people who'd be happy to see me fail. I also learned that I could channel all that negativity into motivation to keep building a business that positively impacts the women it reaches.

LET'S TALK ABOUT YOU

We all learn, get inspired by, and grow from hearing other people's stories. We also all have a story to share that can be positively impactful to other people in our lives and even far beyond. Here are some questions to help you reflect on your own story and how far you've come.

- What stories from other people have impacted your life the most?

- What's a story or experience you can share that you know the people in your life will benefit from?
- What's holding you back from sharing your story or experience?

Sometimes the fear of judgment gets in the way. But as you consider your experiences, focus on the positive impact your stories could have on others—this will outshine all the negativity. Challenge yourself to share your experiences and empower someone else to succeed.

CHAPTER 6

About My
Rich Husband

The idea of having a rich partner goes beyond money. They should be rich in values, character, and integrity.

"You never want to marry a liability, and you never
want to become a liability on any man." Of the few pieces
of dating and marriage advice my dad gave me, this
was the one that stood out the most. He also told me, "It
doesn't matter how rich the man you marry is, you want
to always be able to stand on your own two feet."

Just to be clear. I did not marry a rich man. My husband and I have built our wealth together. And while there is absolutely nothing wrong with marrying rich, that description, "she married rich," is typically used in a way that minimizes any accomplishments that a woman has. Or, it attributes everything that she *has* accomplished in life to the man she married. Of course, I've experienced this firsthand, specifically when it became a topic of discussion after my 2018 *Money* magazine feature that highlighted my $100,000 savings story casually mentioned that I lived in New Jersey with my twins and husband, who is a physician.

Of all the interesting points highlighted throughout the article, I was surprised to find that it was this casual statement that caused the most ruckus. It wasn't the fact that I had achieved a big savings milestone or that I had done it in three and a half years, or even the savings tips and strategies I shared. Instead, it was that I was married to a physician that caused so much contention for certain people.

I remember waking up one day shortly after the magazine issue was released to find that a woman had created a series of posts on her Instagram account discussing me and my "so-called rich husband." She was convinced that the only reason I was able to save any money or build a business was because of my husband's job, and she completely ignored the very clear fact that I was single when I crossed that first big milestone, which was highlighted in the magazine article. She was mad that I had the privilege of being a physician's wife and completely minimized my own personal accomplishments. (This was especially disappointing coming from another woman.)

The comment sections of her posts were full of arguments. Some people felt I didn't belong in the personal finance space because "I married rich" and my life was "easy." Others felt that women should be celebrating other successful women, especially black women, regardless of their marital status or their partners' profession, instead of trying to drag each other down (I 100 percent agree with this). The arguments went on and on.

I was even a guest on a podcast where I was invited to talk about growing my business and about my savings story. During the recording, the podcast host brought up my husband's profession and wanted me to discuss (or perhaps even admit) how much his income had contributed to my success. So, I asked the host, *"As a young woman building my career and achieving big financial milestones, who was I expected to marry?"* After all my hard work and my efforts to get where I was, should I have married an unambitious person with no life vision? Or perhaps a broke ass with no goals? I absolutely and 100 percent do not think so.

When I got married, my husband and I were very much in the early stages of building our careers and assets. He was still in training after just having finished medical school, was barely making any money, and had six figures in student loans from college and medical school. Yup, six figures of debt. As he got out of training, he was intentional about paying his loans. I'm incredibly proud of his accomplishments as a black man, especially when the statistics about being a successful black male are generally unfavorable due to systemic and institutional prejudice and biases.

My husband and I are team players. And as a team, we have always been focused on not just building wealth but also leaving a legacy for our children. As parents to two young black children growing up in America, this is of utmost importance to us. We want to create a legacy of generational wealth that gives our children access to options, the freedom to walk away from what does not serve them, and the ability to give back and help others. As we raise them, our goal is to instill core values in them to help them maintain and pass on this legacy. Although not everyone agrees with this approach of leaving anything to their children, this is the choice we've made for ours based on the opportunities that have been afforded to us by our own parents. I strongly feel that my husband and I are a representation of black excellence. I strive for it and I love to see it.

Of course my husband has contributed to my success. There's no question about that. And I've also contributed to his own success. I married the person who I felt was right for me. But as you know, no relationship is perfect. Mine certainly isn't, and I know firsthand that relationships come with their own fair share of challenges. Despite this, my husband is my ace, my motivator, and my ultimate super-fan, and I'm the same for him. We contribute to each other's success, and I will never apologize for choosing a life partner who is ambitious and successful, and who shares the same goals and vision for our life and our family. Neither should you.

A lot of women feel the societal and family pressure of having to settle down. I definitely felt it. The second I graduated from college, the question I got from every one of my Nigerian aunties was either, *"So. . . when are you getting married? You don't want to get married?!"* or *"Your career?! Are you choosing your career over a husband?!"* and then they would proceed to pray for me to find that future husband—preferably as soon as possible. As a woman coming from a Nigerian background, finding a life partner and getting married is considered a big deal and the pressure is high; most of my Nigerian friends can attest to this as well. But growing up, especially observing my mom and her friends and later as an adult observing other women in society around me, I saw firsthand what happens when women settle.

When women ask me for dating or marriage advice, I always tell them to choose their partner wisely, because partnership (which includes support, flexibility, communication, and mutual respect) in a relationship is so important. So, don't settle. Keep in mind that when I say don't settle, I'm not talking about marrying for money. I'm talking about choosing that person with whom you can create life goals, who has ambition for themselves, and who will support and motivate you while you do the same for them. Choosing that right person will make achieving your goals and building your relationship and life together so much easier.

I can tell you countless stories from women who regret their relationships because they were with the wrong person. Their partners killed their dreams and derailed their goals because they never had a shared vision. I've talked to women who never felt supported by their partners, and as a result gave up on their big ambitions only to find themselves regretful and resentful later on. Granted, some relationships start out great, but people sometimes change, goals deviate, and people disagree. However, it can be easier to get back on the same page if you were both in agreement about your goals and ambitions at the beginning. Some relationships also reach a point where they can no longer be restored. If you get to that point, it's okay if you choose to exit the relationship and move on to a new phase of your life. You want to make the best decisions for yourself and for your personal peace of mind.

I will also say that as women, we should be proud of independently working toward and achieving our own financial goals. Never allow anyone to minimize your accomplishments or shame you for choosing financial wellness for yourself. People are quick to judge a woman for having money. There's always the assumption that someone funds your lifestyle. However, to me, having money as a woman is less about show and more about peace of mind. Whether it's being able to walk away from an abusive or otherwise negative relationship or being about to contribute to your household finances, knowing that you can always stand on your two feet financially and that you can create options for yourself is critical. And so having money is something I will never apologize for.

I dated my fair share of frogs before I found my prince, but I refused to settle until I found him. I had to think deep about what I really wanted in a life partner and what I was willing to tolerate. I knew I could never spend my life with someone who would pull me back or bring me down, especially after having dated that type of person in the past. And the same advice I took for myself is the advice I share with other women.

Yes, I have a rich husband—but it's beyond money. He's rich in values, character, and integrity. He cares deeply about his family, he's an incredible dad, and he's fully vested in our shared vision. To me, this is the real definition of a rich husband, and that's what's most important to me. I'll take this rich husband of mine any day, because he's the best kind.

WHAT I'VE LEARNED

Being married for 11 years, I've learned the true importance of being with the right life partner for me. This is especially true for all the times my husband and I have had to make big decisions, navigate difficult situations, and had major disagreements, all of which are inevitable in any relationship. I've learned that making those big decisions, powering through those difficult times, and apologizing to or forgiving each other when those disagreements occur has only made our relationship stronger because we believe in what we have and we support each other no matter. The relationship my husband and I have is based on mutual respect, support, and love, and we are both vested in making it work.

LET'S TALK ABOUT YOU

Partnership in a relationship is incredibly important—and so is being true to yourself when it comes to who you choose to be with, regardless of what other people think or their opinions about your relationship. Here are some questions to help you reflect on your ideal relationship:

- Who is your ideal partner, and what qualities do they possess?
- What values are most important to you in a relationship? What are your non-negotiables, and what are you willing to be flexible on?
- If you're in a relationship, are you and your partner on the same page when it comes to each other's goals and ambitions? Are you tracking your progress on what you want to accomplish together?
- If you aren't on the same page right now, how can you be intentional about getting on the same page? Be more communicative? Seek counseling?
- What are you committed to doing to build a relationship that works for you both?

Remember, when it comes to relationships, you want to make the best decisions for yourself and for your personal peace of mind. Never settle for second best, because you are worthy of someone who truly honors and uplifts you. If you're single, set the bar high and look for a partner who possesses the qualities and values you wrote down above. If you're in a relationship, work to make sure you and your partner maintain the same values and life goals to achieve your joint dreams.

CHAPTER 7

The Crossroads
to Building an
Impactful Business

The crossroads and the challenges will always show up, but remember why you started what you started, and never forget who you are.

Shortly after quitting my job to run Clever Girl Finance full-time, I found myself really thinking about the type of business I wanted to build long term, and I kept getting stuck on how I was going to do it. My goal was to help women achieve financial wellness by building a business that would positively impact their lives and make a difference. Sure, even if it was slow, I was making progress with figuring out revenue streams and building an audience, but I found myself stuck a lot of times, especially when it came to creating a concrete strategy for growth.

Was I doing things the right way? Was I not doing certain things that I needed to be doing? What expensive mistakes was I getting myself into that I did not yet realize? What could I do to reach more of the women I wanted to help?

I had a bunch of questions I didn't know how to answer, and I constantly felt unsure despite the progress I was making. I had gotten to the point where I knew I needed guidance beyond my skillset and experience if I really wanted to scale. The business books I was reading just weren't cutting it anymore; I needed real-life practical guidance.

So, I decided to leverage the one resource that I knew could help me figure things out—the internet. I got online and started looking for business programs that could help me with strategy and growth. I was looking for classes on entrepreneurship, or anything related. I browsed my local university and community college offerings and, in my search, I stumbled upon a network of volunteer business mentors through SCORE,[1] a nonprofit organization and a resource partner of the US Small Business Administration (SBA). In addition to free webinars and workshops, SCORE offered local events and access to confidential mentorship through their various local chapters. I signed up immediately and scheduled a mentor meeting close to where I lived.

The meeting was at the Small Business offices of a local university, and I was paired with two retired business owners: Matt and William. I didn't know what to expect from this mentorship meeting, so I set my expectations low. When I arrived, however, they were excited to speak with me and learn more about my business. Both mentors had extensive knowledge on growing and scaling their own personal businesses, and now that they were retired, they mentored other business owners. After learning more about my business vision and goals, they put together a whole slew of suggestions for me to review and consider.

From surveying my audience to understand their incentives around financial wellness, to ideas about online advertising and leveraging email marketing, to college and corporate outreach and creating brand awareness. . .I was blown away. They guided me on how to deliver a sales pitch and gave me key tips on how to deliver an engaging presentation. From their guidance, I finally took the leap and started the Clever Girl Finance YouTube Channel and the Clever Girls Know Podcast—ideas I'd been sitting on for ages. I also laid out a plan to document my business processes and determined the contractor and part-time support I needed until the business

---

[1]https://www.score.org/

could afford to hire full-time. All of this came out of one deep-dive session and the email exchanges that followed. I couldn't believe it.

It was from this experience that I realized I needed ongoing guidance, advice, and mentorship. I couldn't truly scale my business the way I wanted to by isolating myself, keeping my blinders on, and allowing my hesitation about doing something to be the reason why I didn't do it. After all, who was keeping me accountable? Yes, I had business peers. But a lot of people I knew had given up on their businesses or were trying to figure things out just like I was. I needed people with experience in strategy, marketing, technology, design, and more to support and guide me and hold me accountable. I needed an advisory board.

This was my first major crossroads in scaling my business. I needed to get out of my own way and get the ongoing support I really needed. So, I started to think about how I would start my advisory board and whom I would ask. While Matt and Will did not offer long term advising, they did encourage me to dig into my network to determine who could help me. My brain was blank. I knew I wanted a diverse board of both men and women, but I had no idea who they would be. However, little did I know that my first two advisors were right in front of me. . .

Dan was the very first advisor I brought on board to Clever Girl Finance, and he also happened to be my former boss's boss at a job I had left a couple years before starting my business. I didn't keep in touch with him, but I did keep in touch with another coworker who had worked directly for Dan and had learned about my business. In one of my conversations with my former coworker, he asked if I had reached out to Dan. My response was, *"No, why should I?"* He went on to tell me about Dan's experience with entrepreneurship and what he was doing now after leaving the company. Dan was a serial entrepreneur and founder of multiple businesses. He had taken a break to step back into the corporate world and since stepping back into entrepreneurship full time, he was also consulting and helping other businesses grow based on his expertise in strategy.

I was hesitant to contact Dan at first. Why would he care about what I was up to now? I didn't work for him anymore. And would he really care about a personal finance business for women? Plus, he probably got a ton of random calls from people pitching businesses and looking for advice. I was sure that if I contacted him, he would find it pretty annoying. I told my former coworker I'd think about contacting Dan, but deep down, I immediately dismissed the idea. Well, a week later, my phone rang. It was Dan on the other end saying, *"I hear you've been up to some cool stuff!"* We ended up having a lengthy but amazing conversation about what I was up to with Clever Girl Finance. Dan was full of advice and had a ton of introductions he wanted to make. He understood my vision and was excited about what I was trying to accomplish, offering to help in any way he could. I took him up on his offer.

Several months later, Dan introduced me to Roshi, a designer and strategist with over 20 years of design innovation experience. Roshi was core to the development of the various elements that make up the Clever Girl Finance brand you see today. So many times she would sit and brainstorm with me on phone calls, Zoom calls, and at coffee shops in Manhattan. Our most memorable session was completely taking over the main tables at the Black Cat Cafe in the Lower East Side with massive Post-it notes and stickies as we were trying to strategize a pitch approach and supporting pitch deck for Clever Girl Finance.

I brought Monique on next—an amazing lady I'd known for years. Our husbands were close friends and she just happened to have recently become the CEO of the longest standing, full-service multicultural marketing and advertising agency in the United States. Monique was full of marketing ideas to help Clever Girl Finance scale and even introduced me to other founders to get advice on growth.

Dan, Roshi, and Monique made up the initial Clever Girl Finance advisory board where they supported me with strategy, design, and marketing. Their guidance was invaluable. I later brought on three additional advisors: Jonathan, who co-founded a nine-figure startup and guides me through growth and day-to-day execution; Maureen, a high-ranking tech executive at one the largest financial institutions in the US who supports our tech initiatives and helps me brainstorm future ideas; and Brent, a business development and sales genius who helps fine-tune our brand partnership strategies. I didn't realize how much I needed to have a dedicated advisory board until I actually had one, and each of my advisors are dear friends who continue to support me and my business today.

Building out my advisory board took a lot of time and effort. I had to develop a relationship with each advisor, prove that my business was worth the time they would dedicate to it, and then formally ask them to come on board. As an introvert, sometimes relationship building can be difficult, but I knew I needed the help. So despite my personal discomfort, I scheduled the meetings and the follow-up meetings, made the phone calls, sent the updates, and had the check-ins. Each time, proving my worth and showcasing the potential of Clever Girl Finance.

While I was building my advisory board behind the scenes, I continued to seek out business programs and courses that could help me expand my knowledge. The SCORE mentoring session had been great, but I wanted to find something that was more in-depth and structured like a business course that I could attend.

Again, during my one of my late-night online searches, I came across the Goldman Sachs 10,000 Small Businesses Program (10KSB)[2] and found out they offered a program in New York City in partnership with the LaGuardia Community College in Queens. The Goldman Sachs 10,000 Small Business Program was a 12-week program focused on helping small businesses grow and scale—and it was completely free to accepted participants. The goal of the 12-week curriculum was for participants to develop a customized growth plan that would help take their business to the next level of growth. Looking at their website, there were several well-known national small businesses in every business niche that had gone through the program. (The US Small Business

---

[2]Goldman Sachs, "10,000 Small Businesses," https://www.10ksbapply.com/

Administration defines a small business as one that has fewer than 1,500 employees.)[3] The particular program I had applied for was supported by the Tory Burch Foundation, which meant that if accepted, my cohort would be entirely made up of women-owned businesses. This made me want to get into the program even more so.

I stayed up late into the night to complete my application that very same day. It didn't matter that it would take me about two hours to get to Queens from where I lived, either by public transportation or car. I didn't care; I'd figure out the logistics of my work schedule and childcare later—plus, I had six months of commuting from Philly to New York every day under my belt. I could do it, and it would be an amazing opportunity if I got accepted.

A few days later, I got an email asking me to schedule an initial phone interview, which I did for the next day. I was asked a few basic questions, including questions about my current business metrics. A couple of days after that, I was invited for an in-person interview. I was so excited.

My interview day came, and I decided to drive into Queens instead of taking public transportation. Unfortunately for me, I got stuck in bad traffic due to an accident and arrived at my interview over two hours late. While I was sitting in traffic, I called the office and left a message and then sent an email explaining why I was running late. I was able to find my interviewer's cell-phone number in my phone and I sent

[3]US Small Business Administration, "Size Standard Tool," https://www.sba.gov/size-standards

him a text as well. I got no responses back and was worried I had blown my chance and wouldn't be seen when I arrived.

Luckily for me, they'd received all my messages and allowed me to be the last interview of the day. I could tell my interviewer was irritated by my lateness and having to conduct a late interview, but I put on my game face and answered every question he grilled me with. He asked me what value my business brought, why I thought I could be successful, what my five-year vision was, and so on. At the end of the interview, he told me they had over 500 applications to review for that cohort and only 30 spots available, and they'd be in touch. Being that I was two hours late, I dismissed the idea of getting accepted into program but consoled myself with the fact that I just had another opportunity to practice my business pitch.

Two weeks later, I got an acceptance letter:

> *Dear Ms. Bola Sokunbi:*
> *Congratulations! On behalf of LaGuardia Community College, we are pleased to inform you that you have been chosen to participate in the 10,000 Small Businesses partnership with the Tory Burch Foundation at LaGuardia Community College. The selection process was quite competitive, as we received many outstanding applications from throughout the New York City tri-state area. You were chosen from this strong pool of candidates and we are hoping that, with your dedication, you will benefit from the program and help to create new jobs and growth.*

I was thrilled! And luckily for me, the hectic commute would be minimized as I only had to be in class once a week on Wednesdays from 8 a.m. to 6 p.m. The rest of the days I would be able to work on take-home assignments from the program while I continued to work on Clever Girl Finance.

My cohort was made up of 30 amazing female CEOs that owned businesses from a wide range of industries. Each week, we'd deep-dive into a particular topic with class activities and individual and group assignments. I learned about identifying growth opportunities for my business, what core metrics and financials to pay attention to, how to develop myself as leader and visionary, how to hire and manage a team, strategic marketing and selling, ideas to find funding and capital, and much more. I also got the opportunity to expand my network and make friends with the women in my cohort, alumni from prior cohorts, and the incredible faculty and staff that supported us throughout the 12-week program.

My Wednesdays were long, commuting four hours roundtrip to attend class with back-to-back lectures and activities. But I loved every moment of the experience—even when I felt like I hated it! I learned so much, I was challenged, and I got to focus on the big picture of where I wanted to take my business. That feeling of being unsure was slowly dissipating.

A few months after completing the Goldman Sachs program, I had the opportunity to apply to Techstars, a renowned mentorship-driven and global tech accelerator program that provides access to funding, fundraising opportunities, workshops, resources, and an incredible alumni community.

Techstars was essentially in the Ivy League of tech accelerator programs. Dan had reached out to me via email, sending me the application link and a brief note that said, *"You should apply to this. It could be an incredible opportunity for you."* Dan had gotten wind of the program from Scott, a good friend of his and a behind-the-scenes advocate of Clever Girl Finance.

At the time, I felt like I needed to take a break after just completing the Goldman Sachs program. But then I looked up the Techstars program and the companies that had been through the accelerator (specifically, the flagship program in New York City where I would be applying to), and I knew that this was one potential opportunity that I could not let pass me by. If I got in, it could be huge. Not only could it be an opportunity to get business capital to help grow Clever Girl Finance, but it could also be an incredible networking and growth opportunity. With companies like ClassPass and Plated on the Techstars portfolio list (at the time of this writing, ClassPass was valued at $1 billion and Plated was acquired for $200 million), and an acceptance rate of 1 percent out of around 17,000 annual program applicants, my hopes of getting admitted were low, like low-in-the-gutter low, but I was going to try anyway.

The fact that I was a solo founder also put me at a disadvantage. According to the reviews I read online, the program preferred companies with multiple co-founders because they could balance the workload of scaling a company. But based on my research, I also knew that many successful solo founders had gone through the program, too, so I applied anyway. Besides, what did I have to lose by applying but a few hours of my day?

The application was due the day after Dan had sent it to me, and it was very involved. It required details around my business vision, my mission, the most recent traction, and why I thought Clever Girl Finance would make a difference. I also had to provide a detailed pitch deck and create a pitch video. I canceled my plans for the day to work on my application, my pitch deck, and to film my video. Luckily for me, the pitch deck came easily because I was able to leverage parts of the growth plan I had created during the Goldman Sachs 10,000 Small Business Program. The video was more challenging, but I put in my best effort, and a few hours later I submitted my application. I got it all done before I could find a reason to talk myself out of it.

To be honest, I didn't expect to hear back at all. But the next day, I got an email from the managing director of the program, Alex, asking if I could meet on videoconference that same day. Of course, I said yes. As soon as I got on the call, Alex said he only had a few minutes to spare but he wanted to make sure he spoke with me, as they had to finalize their decisions that week. After brief pleasantries he said, *"Well, tell me what you've got."*

I don't know about you, but the minute someone tells me they are on a time crunch when I have a big meeting or presentation with them, my nerves set in big time! This happened to me all the time when I worked in corporate America. I can't for the life of me remember what I said. And even though I stumbled over my words, I gave my presentation and remember feeling pretty good about myself. That was until Alex said, *"Yeah, that sounds cool, but I have a better idea. Are you open to hearing it?"*

In my head, I was like, *"Wait, what? Did this guy just say he had a better idea? What's wrong with my idea!?"* My guard came up immediately. I wanted to protect my business, my baby! But at the same time, I also knew I needed to be open to hearing his idea. I didn't want to get to so caught up in protecting my own idea that I let an opportunity pass me by. So, I said, *"Sure, absolutely."*

To provide some context, at this point in time Clever Girl Finance was a content platform (we still are) with a blog and a paid six-month membership program called the Clever Girl Finance Accountability Program where we offered weekly course material and assignments, video calls, and, as the program was titled, accountability. We already had a few hundred women working through the program and ideally, I wanted it to be free because I'd always felt that I didn't want a paywall to be the reason why someone could not get the help they needed to improve their finances. However, at the same time, we needed to earn revenue as a business in order to keep going, so it was necessary to charge a fee for the program. My hope was that I would eventually figure out how to make the program free.

I also had an idea to create a wireframe of a financial app to support our audience with tracking their finances. My pitch to Alex focused on the tech aspect of the platform and building out our financial app. However, Alex's idea for Clever Girl Finance was for the accountability program to be heavily expanded into individual detailed courses converting Clever Girl Finance into a paid course platform enhanced with gamification and using social media as a lead funnel. I told him I thought his idea was great, and while I was not fully convinced that a paid course platform was our only route to scale, I liked the idea of having the opportunity to expand our content offerings. With that, our call ended. I left the call feeling like I hadn't done a good enough job to impress Alex, especially since he'd had his own ideas and suggestions. But as I was processing my thoughts around what happened during the interview, I got an email from him asking me to come into the office the next day for an in-person interview with the broader Techstars team.

It was a mad scramble organizing childcare and planning my commute into New York City for the next day, but I made it there. And before I knew it, I found myself repeating my pitch to Alex and two other members of the Techstars team in a cramped conference room. When I saw them collectively nod and make eye contact, I knew in that moment Clever Girl Finance would be part of the New York City 2018 summer cohort. And true to my gut feeling, I got the acceptance email the very next day. It had been a three-day whirlwind and I couldn't believe that here I was, about to be a Techstars-backed company. The New York City flagship program got thousands of applications for each cohort and Clever Girl Finance was selected to be in one. This was a big freaking deal.

At this moment, however, I found myself at my next crossroad. I needed to decide whether I wanted Clever Girl Finance to be a casual lifestyle business that I built at my own pace and helped women at a small scale or whether I wanted to step all the way out of my comfort zone and take on venture capital from Techstars (while still maintaining majority ownership of Clever Girl Finance) to build a business that pursued big growth, and as a result, could potentially have a large-scale impact on women everywhere. There was the massive Techstars network I could tap into, and I would have access to resources that I otherwise wouldn't have on my own. Making the decision to be backed by venture capital even in this small way was daunting, nerve-racking, scary, and stressful all at the same time. I looked at the curriculum for the 12-week Techstars program that required me to be in New York City every single day with several evening sessions throughout the week and I was completely overwhelmed. When would I see my kids?!

I shared how I was feeling with my husband and he said to me, *"What do you have to lose? We can make this work. It's only for 12 weeks. Plus, the opportunity beyond the 12 weeks is massive."* When it came to my concerns about giving up any equity at all, he quickly broke down the math for me; 100 percent ownership of zero was equal to zero.

I again reflected back to my "why" for starting my business. I knew that accepting the Techstars offer would be the right decision, especially if I wanted to create and participate in change when it came to the narrative of women and money. I was going to do the program, and I was going to pursue building a business that would have large-scale impact. I accepted the offer, made plans for full-time childcare, and planned out my schedule. My goal was to make the effort to spend time with my kids as much as I could. On the days where I had the opportunity to leave early, I would do it and catch up on my assignments on my 1-hour, 20-minute bus ride home or back into the city. I usually left at 5 a.m. before my kids woke up, and most times I got home after my kids had gone to bed. But many times I would wake them up to say hello, give them hugs, and then put them back to bed.

My cohort was made up of 10 companies, and the schedule was exhausting. Each week we had multiple speaker sessions, fundraising talks, team assignments, pitch practices, and networking events. Then there was mentor madness week in the second week of the program, where we gave our pitches to the Techstars program mentors back-to-back all day for a week and got tons of feedback (and even criticism) to implement into our businesses. These mentors were entrepreneurs who had built incredibly successful businesses, subject matter experts, angel investors, and venture capitalists. I talked to over 40 mentors that one week. Starting out with these meetings, I felt like the pressure was on. I was all nerves and was extremely uncomfortable, but with each pitch, it got easier. While all this was going on, I was running the day-to-day of the business. And with the new influx of capital, I was focused on our pivot to expand our course offerings and pursue growth.

During this time, I hired our first brand strategist, Surabhi, who worked with me full time and went through the Techstars program in-person with me. I also hired a part-time community and customer experience manager, Esther, two part-time writers, Ada and Christin, a part-time marketing expert, Hillary, and another part-time financial expert, Melissa, who supported our pivot of building out over 30 personal-finance-related courses. The team grew pretty much overnight, but there was more than enough work to go around.

Surabhi focused on redesigning the entire Clever Girl Finance brand from top to bottom and worked directly with our contracted web developer, illustrator, graphic designer, and course video creators to ensure our brand voice and visuals were properly reflected across the board. She reworked our fonts and colors and established our brand guide. Melissa worked with me on laying out the curriculum for the courses and we both wrote and peer-reviewed the course material. Ada and Christin kept the blog content going as we started to focus on search engine optimization. Esther was focused on audience engagement, and Hillary worked on testing and retesting ad copy for our broader marketing strategy. We had a lot going on, with the biggest investment of time and money going into our rebrand and course development.

One of the best pieces of advice I got during the time as I was expanding the team was from one of my advisors, Roshi, who told me that to scale the way I imagined, I was going to need help. And as I hired help, I needed to empower them to make decisions and execute, so I wouldn't become the bottleneck in the business. Building a team is hard, and I had to let go of everything I was used to doing myself and trust that I had hired good people to help Clever Girl Finance grow and pivot quickly as we went through the 12-week Techstars program.

As the weeks wore on, I got more and more exhausted. The first couple of weeks I made the commute back and forth every day. But as my days got longer and busier, I would spend a few nights a week bouncing between hotels and Airbnb's, depending on what was cheapest and most habitable. The cost hovered somewhere around $200 to $350 a night, which wasn't cheap. But that's the price I had to pay in New York

City since I was booking on a week-to-week basis with little advance time. (I did it this way so I could take the opportunity to go home to my kids and husband whenever I could.)

I stayed in all kinds of places that I'll simply describe as. . . interesting. From the sixth-floor Airbnb that didn't have an elevator where I had to climb up two flights of long steps for each floor to the hotel room that was so old (and I mean *dial TV* old) it had me feeling like I was stuck in *The Twilight Zone*. I remember one particularly frustrating night at an Airbnb in the middle of July on what had to be the hottest day of the year. It was a cramped converted two-bedroom with a kitchen and no living room that should have really been a studio apartment. The shower was in the kitchen and the apartment owner, a lady who I didn't realize would be home, was shuffling all around, trying to make smalltalk. (That's what I got for not reading the fine print while booking my Airbnb at 3 a.m. that prior morning.)

I sat sweating on the bed in my room with a door that didn't quite close all the way and stared at the standing fan that was blowing hot air in my face because, lo and behold, the apartment had no air conditioning. I started crying. I could have been in my own bed in my own house with air conditioning. I could have been there in the morning to take my kids to school and pick them up afterward. Instead, I was here, physically and mentally exhausted in a crappy Airbnb, taking time away from my family to pursue a business dream—did that even make sense? I was ready to quit.

It was too late to go home if I had to be back in the city in just a few hours. So, I picked up my phone and FaceTimed my husband, tears and all, and he talked me off the ledge. We tried to find a hotel, but everything was booked or ridiculously expensive (like $1,000 expensive), and I wasn't going to pay that amount to stay somewhere for six hours. No way. I hated to be a burden on anyone, but I couldn't sleep at that Airbnb. I just couldn't. So, I decided to call my Techstars cohort bestie, Sanj, who lived in Brooklyn with his family to see if he would have mercy on me. Luckily for me, Sanj and his wife had an empty spare bedroom I could crash in, so I packed up my suitcase as quickly as possible, waited for the apartment owner to go to bed, and literally ran away from that Airbnb as fast as I could. I didn't even care that I had paid for it.

A few days later, I caught up with Kalyn, a woman whom I'd become friends with from being in the same cohort at the Goldman Sachs program earlier that year (and who still remains a dear friend years later). As we discussed our progress since completing the program, I shared how I was doing at Techstars and my accommodation nightmare. She said, *"Girl, you can stay with me whenever you need to."* She happened to have an amazing apartment in Tribeca and she gave me her spare keys to crash there anytime. I took Kalyn up on her offer during the times I couldn't find a decently priced hotel (I was done with the cheap crappy Airbnbs). And now that the pitfalls of finding decent accommodation were sorted, I could really focus on finishing the Techstars program.

All of the business-building, pivoting, and pitch practicing we were doing in the program was preparing us for investor madness and demo day—two major opportunities for us as founders in the program to put our best feet forward and seek investment capital that could scale our businesses. Investor madness came first. During this two-week period, each of the 10 companies in my cohort met with and pitched to various angel and venture capital investors with the hopes of raising seed capital to continue to build our businesses. Then demo day came. It was essentially a showcase of all the companies in the program where we pitched our updated and refined business ideas in front of an audience full of investors and the broader Techstars community.

Within Clever Girl Finance, we'd made a ton of progress building out our course platform and growing our social media audience, and I had a solid pitch to deliver. I had over seventy meetings planned over the two weeks of investor madness. It was quite the experience. Despite our being told how difficult and challenging investor pitch meetings could be and how most meetings wouldn't result in an investment commitment, nothing could have prepared me for what I was about to face.

There were the investors I met who were not ready to invest but had really great feedback and wanted to keep in touch as the business grew. There were also the investors who were open about Clever Girl Finance not being a good fit for their portfolio for one reason or the other (e.g., it was the wrong timing, not the right niche or industry for them, etc.). I listened to their feedback, and for the most part, had good conversations.

But then there were the investors I met who made my race and gender the forefront of the conversation and were either racist, sexist, biased, or all of the above. What was most surprising was that some of these investors and venture capital firms were very outspoken about being focused on investing in female and minority founders—but in my pitch meetings, this was so far from the truth.

In one of my first meetings with a minority-focused venture capitalist (VC), the first question the partner asked me as soon as he sat down was, *"So tell me, what white founder are you trying to copy?"* and then he laughed. He appeared to be joking, but I didn't find it funny. At all. I was here to talk business, not to be patronized, and so I asked him, *"Why would I need to copy a white founder?"* I kept it professional, gave my pitch, and kept it moving. But that was just the beginning.

As I progressed with my meetings, the question, *"Are you married?"* was basically a standard, and I received many comments, feedback, and questions like the following:

> *"You shouldn't wear your wedding ring to meetings. It tells people that you might have too much going on in your personal life and might not be able to commit to building a serious business"* and *"You should wear high heels and lipstick when meeting specific male investors. They'll take you more seriously."*
>
> –From a tenured female founder and angel investor.

> *"What does your husband think about you becoming a CEO?"*
>
> –From a male investor who cut me off mid-sentence.

"Don't ever talk about your kids. It's too much baggage."

–From a male angel investor, right after he asked the question, *"Do you have kids?"*

"What you're building is too techy for black women. You need to bring it down to their level. They don't really use computers like that."

–From a minority-focused VC.

"You should smile more."

–From a male VC, right after I talked about the depressing statistic that women of color have a median net worth of between $100 and $200, depending on their minority demographic.[4]

"Your business is a gimmick. Why the focus on women or women of color? Everyone in America has equal opportunities."

–From a female angel investor.

I found myself going to meetings and asking myself, *"What would Jesus do?"* In some meetings, it took every ounce of my being to keep it professional. And most times, instead of having a constructive conversation, I found myself defending my gender, my race, and the value of my business. This experience was not unique to me. There were three other

---

[4]Andrea Flynn, *Justice Doesn't Trickle Down: How Racialized and Gendered Rules Are Holding Women Back* (Roosevelt Institute and the Ms. Foundation for Women, May 22, 2017), https://rooseveltinstitute.org/wp-content/uploads/2020/07/RI-Justice-Doesnt-Trickle-Down-201705.pdf

companies with female founders in my cohort, and each of them complained of being patronized in investor meetings. My male founder counterparts were not asked about their marital status. Neither were they told to smile more or not wear their wedding rings. They were also not told to dumb things down or wear high heels and lipstick to look attractive to investors. The patronization was ridiculous—so ridiculous that I had to let the Techstars team know. I was told that my complaints and the complaints of the other female founders would be added to the investors feedback, and that was pretty much it. There was no so surprise there. I wasn't the first female founder to go through this, and I certainly wouldn't be the last. Investors came with money and that was the bottom line, complaints or no complaints. But regardless, I let my voice be heard and then I kept it moving.

However, despite the ridiculousness of these nonsensical comments and the people behind them, there were some lessons for me to learn. First of all, I needed to grow thicker skin. Like, alligator-thick skin. If there's anything I knew for sure by now, it was that in the business of building a business, thick skin is a must. One cannot survive without it. Investor madness hammered that in. I realized that some people just have problems, and it's not my job to help them solve those problems. I'm also not anyone's pushover, and I won't pretend to be someone I'm not. So, I was polite and matter of fact about my opinion or disagreement, all while killing them with kindness. And that was it.

I also wore my wedding rings to every meeting (and I shined them up just before so they'd be all nice and sparkly!). If anyone asked me about my kids, I told them all about them. And I'll be damned if I was wearing high heels or lipstick to impress some random man because I wanted him to take me seriously.

Second, I constantly reminded myself to never forget why I started what I started—especially at those incredibly trying meetings. I couldn't afford to let anyone's bias diminish my vision or my focus. Clever Girl Finance was making an impact and changing lives. I wasn't going to settle for anyone's stupid ideas like *"Black women don't use computers."* I was going to stay focused on my focus.

I got through every single one of those investor meetings and I pitched my heart out at demo day. While my male counterparts raised millions of dollars, I raised zero capital from investor madness, demo day, and the 20 or so additional investor meetings I had after the Techstars program concluded (I had over 90 meetings in total). Initially, this was challenging for me. I was extremely disappointed. I felt like I had failed. I'd seen male founders raise hundreds of thousands to millions of dollars on an idea with no traction or revenue, only to shutter the business a few short months or years later. Yet, here I was with traction and revenue but zero investment dollars to show for it.

The truth is, however, that women receive only around 2 to 3 percent of the billions of venture capital that's invested annually—and my business was no exception to that poor statistic. In fact, *Harvard Business Review* shared that in 2019, 2.8 percent of funding went to women-led startups while in 2020, that number fell to 2.3 percent.[5] Quite a

---

[5] https://hbr.org/2021/02/women-led-startups-received-just-2-3-of-vc-funding-in-2020

disturbing fact, especially given that women make up over 40 percent of US business owners.

However, my lack of investment capital didn't sum up my Techstars experience. If anything, it was a silver lining. By being in the program, I got to hire an amazing team and expand our incredible platform that is helping women every single day. I grew my network tremendously and got exposed to opportunities I would've never had access to otherwise, and there is always someone I can call through the Techstars alumni network if I ever have an issue.

Not raising capital, while disappointing at first, allowed me to get creative with generating revenue, and was really a blessing in disguise. It meant I could do things on my own terms at my own pace as the majority shareholder in my business. After this experience, I focused on creating backup funds for my business, so no one can ever tell me what to do. I've become my own majority investor. And as a result, I don't have an investors board to worry about, and I don't have to deal with the pressures of one, either. I've seen too many instances where a founder's vision has been derailed because they took on too much capital and gave up too much ownership. Instead of pursuing their own vision and dreams, they got caught up in having to deliver to the demands of their investors and pursue growth at all costs. I've seen founders pushed out of their own businesses because their goals and their investors' goals no longer aligned. That's the last thing I wanted for myself. Techstars gave me just enough capital as a dormant investor to get to the next level and that was perfect. I'm now in a position where I can pay back every investment dollar received if I need to without any impact to the overall business. This leverage is incredibly important to me. Today, I get emails from investors all the time as Clever Girl Finance has grown and gotten on their radar. However, I'm extremely grateful to be in a position where I don't need to take on any new investment unless I absolutely want to.

As Techstars concluded, I received my first book deal for *Clever Girl Finance: Ditch Debt, Save Money, and Build Real Wealth* from my current publisher, John Wiley & Sons Inc., aka Wiley, officially making me a published author upon its completion a year later.

A year earlier, I was a couple of chapters into writing the book, before the Goldman Sachs program and before Techstars, but I had put it on hold to go through those programs. I had not thought very far ahead as to how I would publish it or pitch it to any book publishers. It was simply a pet project and a bucket-list item I was taking my time to complete. I told myself I would figure out how I would publish it later.

I started thinking about picking up book writing again after I finished the Techstars program, and I mentioned that I was writing a book to my advisor, Dan. He said that if I was ever interested in having it published, he might know some people he'd gone to college with who went on to work in publishing that I could talk to about crafting a pitch. He'd just need to do some research to determine where they were—20-something years later! So, I said okay, not thinking much of it.

While Dan was doing his research, Wiley had learned about me and Clever Girl Finance from our media features and had done their own research to learn more about the brand. When they first reached out, it was a preliminary introduction call to gauge my interest in potentially writing a book with them. I wanted to put it off and find a way to delay the conversation because I was so tired after such a hectic year, but it was another incredible opportunity and I would have been crazy not to pursue it.

The book I'd already started writing would fit perfectly with the idea Wiley had, and they are a well-known and reputable publisher. (Wiley publishes the extremely popular *For Dummies* book series, among thousands of other very successful consumer, professional, and academic books.) It would be an opportunity to have a book in bookstores and with major book retailers. To me, this was huge, especially thinking back on that experience I had years ago at the bookstore trying to find a personal finance book for women by a woman.

Coincidently, Dan had found and reached out to a college buddy who used to work at Wiley to learn more about how they worked with authors, and it seemed very positive. I also told my advisor, Roshi, about the opportunity, and based on her design innovation experience, she asked me to start thinking about what the cover would look like. She suggested I use this cover to set the foundation for a future book series. I didn't have a completed book and hadn't even signed the book contract yet, but Roshi was thinking way ahead of me— and she was so right! (Honestly, there's nothing like having advisors who will go all out to see you succeed.)

I agreed to go ahead with the process of publishing my first book with Wiley, and I worked with my lawyer to negotiate my contract. Then I built out my book outline and set aside a minimum of an hour a day, either before my kids woke up or after their bedtime, to write. Some days I'd stare at the screen, writer's block in full effect, and only manage to write a few words. Other days, I had paragraphs spilling out of me. I hired a developmental editor who coached me on how to improve my writing so I could create a solid body of work. Several months later, I submitted my first manuscript.

When people ask me for advice on writing a book, I share exactly what worked for me: create an outline to keep you on track, plan out your writing schedule, and get a second set of experienced eyes on your writing to give you feedback (even if you might not always like what they have to say!).

Clever Girl Finance: Ditch Debt, Save Money, and Build Real Wealth was released on June 25, 2019, and was the first of what is now a three-part Clever Girl Finance book series. Writing that book was an incredible opportunity with which to close out the year, and it helped tremendously to build awareness for the brand.

As I look back, this particular year with Goldman Sachs, Techstars, and signing my first book deal was game changing. Every time I thought I was ready to take a break, something else appeared that I couldn't say no to. I stepped all the way out of my comfort zone to build a business of impact with the support of an incredible team. I took advantage of the opportunities that came my way despite my discomfort, and I leveraged those opportunities for a greater good, despite the biases and prejudice. Building a business is really hard, and, on my ongoing journey to building this business, I've had to stop and ask myself many times if it's worth it. The answer has always been a resounding yes. This is simply because the work I'm doing—supported by an incredible team and amazing advisors—is helping change the lives of women everywhere, and this means everything to me.

This is me choosing to prosper, but on my own terms. When other founders and business owners ask me for advice, especially when they reach their own crossroads, I always tell them this: building a meaningful business is worth the tears and sacrifice—and being able to do it on your own terms can make all the difference when it comes to the motivation you need to keep going. The crossroads and the challenges will always show up, but always remember why you started what you started and remember who you are. I've found this advice valuable not just in building my business but as I carry on in my journey through life.

WHAT I'VE LEARNED

As I shifted from my career into building and running Clever Girl Finance full-time, I was terrified. My career provided a sense of security and I was putting that aside to pursue a passion and a dream I wasn't sure would work out, but, in the process, I learned some valuable lessons. I learned that I needed to step outside of my comfort zone but I could also think objectively and create actionable plans to help manage my fears. I learned how to handle rejection without feeling minimized or allowing other people to minimize my efforts and potential. And I also learned that although things might not always work out as I hoped (for instance, raising investment capital), there is always a silver lining and alternative opportunities as long as I don't give up.

LET'S TALK ABOUT YOU

As you grow in your career, business, or personal life, stepping outside of your comfort zone is necessary. Yes, it's scary. But this is where the magic happens. This is where you turn all those dreams and what-ifs into reality. Here are some questions to help you reflect on the opportunities that may be waiting for you just outside of your comfort zone:

- What opportunities have presented themselves to you that would require you to step outside of your comfort zone? Did you take them on?
- If you did, how did you adjust to the discomfort? If you didn't, what specifically held you back?
- Knowing what you know now, how can you better prepare to step outside of your comfort zone to open the doors to new opportunities and achieve your goals?

One way to get comfortable with stepping outside of your comfort zone is to create a list of questions you ask yourself each time you are presented with a new opportunity. Some of these questions could be:

- When I'm old, will I look back and wish I had pursued this opportunity?
- Am I hesitant to do it because I'm afraid to take the leap or because I know it's not a good fit for me?
- What's the worst thing that could happen if I pursued this opportunity? What's the best thing that could happen?

CHAPTER 8

Imposter Syndrome, Mental Health, and Other Personal Challenges

Prioritize the important things in your life, give yourself the grace to accept that doing your best is enough, and remind yourself why you're amazing.

Like many things in life, being a business founder, business owner, business creator, whatever you want to call it, is hard. Like, really hard. And I learned very quickly that the experience can be really hard on your mental health as well. I left the security and comfort of a consistent income, my potential career trajectory, and my 401(k) contributions to step out into the crazy world of business because I wanted to try to build something worthwhile. So many people questioned my decision to quit my job and thought that perhaps I was going through a phase, and honestly, sometimes so did I. Was I crazy?

In addition to dropping my job security, there was the burden and overwhelm of trying to figure out how to actually build Clever Girl Finance, which sometimes felt like the burden of the entire world was on my shoulders. There were also the hideously depressing metrics about business startup failures, which were a constant reminder that I was most likely to fail even when I was making progress (I'll clue you in—you have a 50/50 chance of being around after five years of business. . . and that's the polite stat). And then there was my imposter syndrome that constantly had me questioning my abilities and doubting myself.

I also had very young twins who at the time didn't give a damn about my business. If you asked my daughter, she would tell you Mommy works on a platform. My son would tell you Mommy is a businesswoman. But when it really came down to it, they couldn't care less because my platform and my business meant work, and work meant less time with Mommy, and that was no fun. This was my life. Waking up at 5 a.m. to get a head start on some work, make school lunches, get dressed, and then get my kids dressed. Then it was school drop-off, a workout if I could fit it in (I rarely did), and then straight to the home office for more work and meetings. Later in the day, it was school pickup, kid's activities, dinner for the family, bath time and bedtime for my kids, and then I'd do a bit more work. Sometimes with my work load it felt like I never actually quit my full-time job or photography side hustle. Whether you are a mom who works full time for a company or a mom who's running her own business, this hectic schedule is the reality for many of us. Life is busy and exhausting.

Yes, starting out on my journey to build a business was nerve-racking, but it was nerve-racking and exciting all at the same time—especially in those early days.

Exciting because it was my chance to go out and build something amazingly incredible and impactful.

Nerve-racking because, well, what if it was just a giant, massive, horrible mistake?

Exciting because stepping out into the unknown was like a burst of fresh air in my life—but it also could've been equated to standing outside naked in the freezing cold. . . (It really depends on how you look at it).

Nerve-racking because who was I to think I could do this? (Hello, imposter syndrome.)

Exciting because I got to be my own boss and set my own schedule.

Nerve-racking because I needed to make money, and make it fast.

Exciting because I had a chance to be just like the featured founders in the glossy magazines and in big media throwing around fancy business lingo like product-market fit, lifetime value, cost of acquisition, retention, and conversion rates. . .

Nerve-racking because did anyone really give a &^$% about what I was building or my fancy terms? And wait a minute. . .was I a terrible mom?!

In those early days—after the excitement had worn off and the reality started to set in—I started to experience many realizations. For instance, I started to agree with those people who thought perhaps I was, indeed, out of my mind. I most certainly realized by this point that "overnight success" was a myth. I had also reached the point where I considered getting a "real job" almost every other day. I often thought about going back to beg for my old one, and I may have even gone onto Indeed.com one late night and applied to 60 jobs in one sitting because I was so over building a business. Ah, the mental anguish. Being a founder was hard. I mean, it still is. But back then, it was extra, extra hard. That being said, I've learned a few things on my journey that have allowed me to pursue my life as a business owner on my own terms. Things that in turn have helped me manage my mental and emotional health, as well as that annoying imposter syndrome. I want to share those things with you now.

Let's start with the all-so-popular idea of work–life balance. Wikipedia defines work–life balance as "*the state of equilibrium in which demands of personal life, professional life, and family life are equal."*[1] Umm, yeah, that's a lie. Work–life balance is a lie. There's no balance. It's called making it work, however you make it work. There's no background music playing over my day showcasing me as the perfect wife, mom, entrepreneur, and Superwoman like you see in the movies. It's simply me making my life work every day. And in order to make things work, I have learned to prioritize what matters most, put some things on the back burner, and let some things just fall off completely. To hell with the balancing act.

I used to be the mom and wife who wanted to have the perfect meal on the table at dinner time every night, even after an insanely busy day. I used to be the mom who ironed all the clothes perfectly and organized the closets and toys catalog-style. I was Superwoman, all day, every day. Even when I was super-tired. It didn't take long for the real overwhelm and stress to set in. Being Superwoman was no longer sustainable, but neither was being stressed out. I couldn't be stressed out and still be trying to make it all work at all costs. After bouts with severe migraines and migraine-induced vertigo, I realized I need to change my approach and let go of trying to balance everything to achieve "a state of equilibrium."

For instance, there are about six meals I cook really well. My family loves these meals. They don't take me forever to make, and I can batch cook and freeze portions for later. Want to eat something else? Looks like we'll be ordering in. I hire childcare for day-to-day life and no longer just for when I have to leave home super-early or have to travel. They help

[1]https://en.wikipedia.org/wiki/Work%E2%80%93life_balance

me with laundry and tidying up, too. This frees me up to spend more quality time with my children. Childcare not available? That laundry is just going to pile up until I get around to it, and I'm okay stepping on Legos. I also have a cleaning service that comes to clean my house, because I'd rather spend my free time on the weekends with my husband and kids than worrying about cleaning tasks and scrubbing the bathroom floor (or arguing with my husband about cleaning). I sometimes reschedule or completely cancel business meetings because my kids have a recital, class party, or I just want to pick them up from school and go buy donuts, full stop.

Yes, my business is important, but my family is non-negotiable. I delegate a lot (I will not be the bottleneck), and I rely on my amazing team to get work done for my business. Some days I don't answer calls, reply to emails, check Instagram, or respond to text messages because I want to spend time with my family or because I don't want to deal with anything or anyone else (Hello, introverted Bola!). I no longer try to be Superwoman or chase the mythical idea of "work–life balance" or "perfect equilibrium." I give myself the grace to not be all the things all the time. I make it work however I make it work, and I'm 100 percent fine with that.

Next up is my mental health. As I've already mentioned, if you want to survive in business, you need to grow thick skin. However, this doesn't mean you ignore your emotions. In fact, I've learned that fully embracing the emotions I'm feeling as opposed to trying to ignore them or push them aside really helps me manage my mental health. Sometimes that means I just need to take that deep sigh and have a good cry. It's inevitable that you'll get feedback you hate. Your customers will hate your product. Investors will tell you your business sucks. Friends will think you're going through a phase. You'll be too broke to buy that thing you really want, when if you had a "real job" it wouldn't even be a question. So yes, sometimes, crying is necessary. However, just because it's okay to cry doesn't mean you let it become a crux. After all, crying gives you red puffy eyes, which makes in-person meetings and videoconferences with your team, mentors, advisors, or investors really hard to do. Crying also causes headaches (sometimes even migraines), makes you to want to crawl back into bed forever (and ever), makes you feel sad and depressed, and in very many instances, wastes so much of your time.

When I find myself getting into a crying rut (because I'm absolutely not immune to this), I try to find ways to make myself smile or laugh. Sometimes it's by thinking about how stupid what I'm crying over really is, playing with my kids, finding something good on Netflix to take my mind off the crap, or indulging in some self-care. Laughing instead of crying means I can attend my meetings and videoconferences like a boss. It means I can take the feedback (bring it on) and be in the right state of mind to consider it and respond. It also means I can get back to work building my amazing business instead of nursing a hideous headache. This approach isn't foolproof, but it works for me most times.

And finally, let's talk about that damn imposter syndrome, which pops up at the most inconvenient times, making you feel less than good enough, uncapable, and unworthy. It promotes that negative self-talk and self-judgment that can keep you stuck in a perpetual cycle of pity parties and "woe is me." I've experienced imposter syndrome a ton and let me tell you, it never goes away. It's always right there, the annoying uninvited guest, rearing its ugly head just before every milestone and every accomplishment. However, I've come up with ways to tackle it and minimize its impact in my life. I've found that sharing my mindset challenges with my husband, my business advisors, my friends, and my business peers can be incredibly helpful, especially when it comes to reminding me that I'm being totally irrational with those thoughts of feeling less than who I am.

I also started keeping a list of all my business and life accomplishments (no matter how small) because they remind me how far I've come and what I'm capable of doing. Things like hiring my first full-time employee, becoming a Goldman Sachs 10KSB alum, becoming a Techstars portfolio company, having a two-page spread in *Money* magazine—these are all on my list. I wrote down being at my kids' Kindergarten graduation, attending their class plays, and ringing the opening bell at the New York Stock Exchange when Clever Girl Finance was selected to participate in the Citi Open Innovation Challenge. I've written down every media opportunity I've had: *Forbes, CNBC, Fast Company, Business Insider, Black Enterprise, The Washington Post, Time*, the *BBC World Service, Fortune, The Chicago Tribune*, and many, many more. I wrote down being featured in a dedicated segment on *Good Morning America* (they came to film at my house!), being on the *Ryan and Kelly Show*, and my list goes on and on. Plus, there's the completion of this book, which will make me a four-time published author. *Clever Girl Finance: Ditch Debt, Save Money and Build Real Wealth, Grow Your Money*, and *The Side Hustle Guide* are all books I authored with my name on the front cover. Yes. That was me. Take that, imposter syndrome! I don't believe your lies. I've got the real facts!

Most importantly, I've stopped comparing myself and my journey to that of other people, because I realize that approach is a fool's errand. I am uniquely me on my own unique journey. Yes, other people are doing much more amazing things in their lives and their businesses right now, but their journeys and paths are much different than mine. And my faith in God and the knowledge that there's enough room for everyone to succeed keeps me grounded. I constantly remind myself that comparison is the thief of joy, and why would I do that to myself when I've accomplished so much and have so much to be joyful for?

The truth is, no amount of preparation can get you totally ready for the rollercoaster that is the business-building journey. Trust me, I know. There's also no perfect blueprint to being a CEO and wife, mom, caregiver, or whatever other life roles you already have as you build a business. It's all about making it work in the way that works for you, giving yourself the grace to accept that doing your best is enough, and reminding yourself why you're amazing and more than capable of achieving success.

WHAT I'VE LEARNED

Imposter syndrome, insecurities, overwhelm, anxiety. . .these are all things I deal with on a regular basis. I've learned that I can't avoid them, and pretending they don't exist in my life is not helpful, especially when it comes to my mental health. So instead, I've learned to accept and work through them whenever they rear their ugly heads. I've learned not to allow myself to get stuck behind my own limiting thoughts. I remind myself of what I've accomplished, what my goals are, and what I know I'm capable of. I assess myself and my past actions for opportunities to improve, I lean on my support system especially when things get tough, and all the while I keep moving forward.

LET'S TALK ABOUT YOU

Imposter syndrome is real, and when we experience it, it can be incredibly limiting. But it doesn't have to be. Here are some questions to help you reflect and get past it.

- In what specific situations in your life has imposter syndrome reared its head, and how did you handle it?
- How do you approach the feeling of being an imposter or incapable today?
- What actions can you take to help tackle any imposter syndrome you might feel in the future so you can continue to focus on achieving your goals?

While feeling imposter syndrome may not go away permanently, it doesn't have to limit you. Reflect on your accomplishments and successes so far, no matter how small you think they are. Reflect on every difficult situation and how you overcame them. Focus on the positive side of every situation you are presented with. Doing these things will remind you of how capable you are, regardless of what the little voice in your head is saying. Remember, there's no perfect blueprint to living your life and doing your best to accomplish your goals. It's all about making it work in the way you can best make it work, knowing that you have what it takes to succeed.

CHAPTER 9

The Year 2020

2020 was painful, but a reminder that life is worth living, even more so authentically and on your own terms.

Like many, I stepped into 2020 with big hopes and aspirations for the start of a brand-new decade. Little did we know that 2020 would be a year that would turn the entire world completely upside down. I remember having to travel for a women's conference I was speaking at in Oxford, Mississippi, at the end of February 2020 and seeing the headlines about the pandemic on the news as I waited for my flight. It was quite unnerving. There were even a few people wearing masks in the airport, which made me feel even more unsettled. I decided that maybe I needed to buy a mask for myself, but no one was selling them in the airport concession stores, so I bought a bottle of hand sanitizer instead. The unsettling feeling stayed with me all through my flight. I wasn't sure what to do at first, but once I arrived at the conference, it was just a regular day where everything seemed normal, and I forgot all about the uneasiness I'd felt earlier. Two weeks later we went into a panicked lockdown across the country and as the days, weeks, and months passed, we all began to feel the real and devastating impact of the COVID-19 pandemic.

Overnight, things got crazy for everyone. Schools were closed with no plans in place for remote learning. Employees were sent home. Grocery stores were overwhelmed with demand but not enough supply, and then there was the terrible, terrible news. The job loss reports were staggering as businesses shuttered. COVID-19-related cases and deaths were rising, medical experts were just trying to determine the symptoms, and a medical solution was nowhere in sight.

I was home alone with my twins trying to manage my fears about everything that was happening. I was also trying to manage my business while keeping them occupied and attempting to figure out homeschool like millions of other mothers and families. As the weeks progressed, my twins' preschool created packages parents could pick up to help them continue their Kindergarten learning at home. I was exhausted, but we were the lucky ones. I'd heard of so many schools—especially in inner city neighborhoods where remote learning was not an option due to the lack of funds— where some teachers were paying out of pocket to gather materials to share with their students.

As medical professionals, my husband, mom, and two sisters-in-law were all going into work at their various hospitals as the pandemic raged on, and the news of people we knew who'd died from the COVID-19 virus started to surface. I was beyond stressed and afraid of what could possibly happen to my family members and friends who were essential workers, risking their lives every single day by going to work. Every day I woke up and tried to manage my sanity and create a sense of emotional well-being for my kids (who were also worried, even though they didn't fully understand what was going on). I found myself getting extremely overwhelmed, and I just cried. I cried from navigating the emotions of knowing my husband and family members were out of the house working with a virus on the rampage. I cried working through my business. I cried trying to navigate homeschool, trying to navigate kids, trying to keep everybody happy, and trying to create a sense of normality. In between letting myself have a good cry and batch cooking, I found my coping mechanism.

I eventually figured out a plan that worked for me—I would let my kids stay up later at night so they would wake up later in the morning. Then, I would wake up at 5 a.m. (my favorite time of the morning, it seems), just when my husband was leaving for work. I would try to get as much work done as possible before my kids got up and I had to sort out breakfast and homeschooling.

As personal finance was a hot media topic, I started to get a ton of media and television opportunities. I could have said no because, well, life was hard, and then complained later about a missed opportunity. But instead, I got on the phone with different producers as my kids screamed in the background and said, *"Yes, I'll do it! But by the way, I have young kids,"* and *"Yes, we can do it before my kids wake up."* So, there I was, many times before 6 a.m., with my hair combed, makeup on, and my webcam set, making the choice to take advantage of the opportunities I was presented with and aiming to make it work as best as I could.

And for the media opportunities that needed me to be live during the day when my kids were awake, there were a number of them where my children were the background noise and even one where my twins flat-out howled. Together. The. Entire. Time. I kept a straight face, did my interview, and kept it moving. I found comfort in knowing I was not the only one. On a couple occasions, I got to hear a co-guest's child crying in the background and another time when a co-guest had to hang up while on live TV because her kids just weren't having it. That was the new normal.

You certainly don't need me to remind you how incredibly difficult 2020 was for all of us. And despite my own personal trials, so many people had much worse experiences that I did.

People were struggling financially, and so many people had to deal with the devastation of losing loved ones. And even as things started to improve and the lockdown rules were lifted, schools still remained virtual or closed. As a result, so many mothers felt the blow of not being able to return to work even if their jobs were still there because they didn't have anyone to help watch their young children. This meant the continued loss of income for so many women. And the bad news went on and on.

In addition to the impact of the pandemic, we navigated a racial injustice reckoning triggered by the unlawful murder of George Floyd and so many countless other black men and women before him. I had to have difficult conversations and set expectations about ongoing racism in America with my young children as they saw the news headlines and watched the protests on TV.

Honestly, we all deserve trophies for our resilience through the crazy year, and I have to say an extra, extra special thank-you to all the frontline and health-care workers, teachers, other essential workers, and small business owners who were out there working despite everything that was happening. Personally, I was so ready to put 2020 behind me—and I'm certain you were, too. But despite what 2020 was, there is still so much that I personally have to be grateful for. Specifically, that I'm alive, my family is well, and I'm here writing this book.

From a business perspective back in March 2020, one week after the lockdown was announced (on March 19, to be specific), we decided to make the entire Clever Girl Finance course platform completely free. We did this to support our community of women who were anxious to get their finances together. There was so much panic with that initial lockdown with people not being able to go to work or earn money. People were worrying about how they were going to pay their bills and support their families. People were worrying about their health. And on top of that, there was so much unknown about the virus. Making the platform free was the least we could do with everything going on.

Having a completely free platform was something I'd always wanted to do because I'd always felt unsettled about charging people who came to us with a real need for financial wellness but were unable to pay. Figuring out the business finances to support such a decision, however, had proven tricky, especially when it came to recurring income. However, in that moment with the pandemic raging, making our courses free was one way I knew we could support our community through an incredibly difficult season. Within a few minutes of discussing things as a team, it was decided. Our courses would be free. . .permanently. We sent out an email, all payments were turned off, and we issued refunds to those who had recently paid for a course. If there ever was a time for us to step up and take a risk to help others, which is what our business mission is all about—helping others—it was right then.

The pivot cost Clever Girl Finance a lot financially, as our revenue took a significant hit. I had to rely on the cash buffer I'd built from putting aside a percentage of all earnings over the last few years to support our expenses and make sure the team was paid once we cut off that income stream. We had basically pushed ourselves off a ledge, taking a leap of faith that it would all work out as we supported our community. However, it was also the perfect opportunity for us as a business to get out of our comfort zone, think hard, strategize, and look for new opportunities. And while we strategized and restructured our approach to how we would replace this revenue stream, big opportunities came our way as a result of making our courses free. The pivot led to a massive growth of our community. And within three months, we'd not only replaced the course platform revenue but we'd *tripled* the earnings we were making from our courses—all thanks to several new partnerships. In return, these partnerships led to other opportunities of recurring income, and for that I am extremely grateful.

As the decision was made to make our platform free, we realized we also needed to figure out how we could do more to support our community. We were getting devastating emails and direct messages from women who had lost their jobs and were unable to put food on the table to feed their kids or buy formula to feed their babies. This broke my heart—especially because so many of the women in need in our community were either just starting their financial wellness journey or had been devasted by loss or major financial changes in their households. We looked at our budget and carved out some money to give away grocery store gift cards on a weekly basis via Instagram to members of our community. It was not a ton of money, but it was something that would help a few people. Our plan was to share posts that we wanted to buy groceries for a few families and select people randomly from the comments to send the gift cards to. However, once we made our first giveaway post, we were overwhelmed with messages from other women in our community and beyond who wanted to help out as well by donating additional grocery store gift cards. As a result, we were able to pull together thousands of dollars' worth of $50 and $100 gift cards that helped so many women. This show of love and support reinforced the value of community and why what we do at Clever Girl Finance to create a community focused on financial wellness truly matters. I pray for continued blessings on every single person who made a gift card donation to support another woman in need during that time.

The pandemic also reinforced why it was incredibly important for Clever Girl Finance, as a business, to have multiple streams of income. We had a few different streams of income in place prior to the pandemic, but with the pandemic in full swing and seeing its negative impact on so many small businesses, it became a priority to grow our existing streams and expand into new ones. And that was something we were forced to focus on as we took our leap of faith.

As we settled into our new focus, I was contacted about an opportunity to write a statement for the record in support of a hearing that focused on the challenges women and minorities faced when it came to accessing financial services and capital,[1] especially as the pandemic raged. This was (and still is) an issue very close to my heart and one that I had

---

[1]SBE Council, "Testimony Before U.S. House Financial Services Committee, Subcommittee on Diversity and Inclusion: Access to Capital Challenges During the Pandemic," July 9, 2020, https://sbecouncil. org/2020/07/09/access-denied-challenges-for-women-and-minority-owned-businesses-accessing-capital-and-financial-services-during-the-pandemic/

firsthand experience with during my own initial attempts to raise capital for Clever Girl Finance, so I was more than happy to write a statement as a way to use my voice in contribution to calling out these challenges and effect change.

The hearing took place on July 9, 2020, and was held by the Subcommittee on Diversity and Inclusion chaired by Congresswoman Joyce Beatty under the House Committee on Financial Services chaired by Congresswoman Maxine Waters. My statement for the record was as follows:

STATEMENT FOR THE RECORD

The challenges women and minorities face in accessing financial services during COVID-19

July 7th, 2020

Honorable Chairwoman, Joyce Beatty,

House Committee on Financial Services,

Subcommittee on Diversity and Inclusion,

Chairwoman Beatty and Members of the Committee and Subcommittee, thank you for the opportunity to write a statement for the record on the challenges women and minorities face in accessing financial services and capital during the COVID-19 pandemic to be presented before the Subcommittee on Diversity and Inclusion of the U.S. House Committee on Financial Services on July 9th, 2020.

My name is Bola Sokunbi. I'm the Founder and CEO of Clever Girl Finance Inc. While I come from a Technology and Strategy background, previously working for Fortune 500 companies like Comcast and Time Warner Cable, my career path transitioned into financial wellness, specifically for women.

This decision was based on my personal experiences trying to find financial resources to support my needs as a woman of color and finding that these resources for women like me were few and far between. Today, Clever Girl Finance is one of the largest personal finance platforms for women in the United States with an audience base primarily made up of women of color.

As the COVID-19 pandemic continues to rage on, the long-standing systemic social and health inequities have put many minorities at increased risk of illness from this virus. However, this is just one issue that this pandemic has brought to the forefront. Unemployment rates are currently at 11.1% up from 3.8%[2] prior to the pandemic with female unemployment higher on average. Business closures are at record highs with a 41% decline in black business owners and a 32% decline in Latino business owners compared to a 17% decline in white business owners.[3]

Needless to say, while this pandemic has been hard-hitting to everyone, people of color are bearing the brunt of it.

[2]Rakesh Kochhar, "Unemployment rose higher in three months of COVID-19 than it did in two years of the Great Recession," Pew Research Center, June 22, 2020, https://www.pewresearch.org/fact-tank/2020/06/11/unemployment-rose-higher-in-three-months-of-covid-19-than-it-did-in-two-years-of-the-great-recession/
[3]"Minority Small Business Owners Harder Hit by Pandemic Closures: 'A Total Nightmare,'" CBS Morning News, June 22, 2020, https://www.cbsnews.com/news/coronavirus-minority-small-business-owners-pandemic-closures/

In efforts to financially survive this pandemic, many unemployed people are turning to starting a business as a way to generate income and many businesses are seeking capital to stay afloat. Unfortunately, the lack of starting capital and the inability of women and minorities to access business capital from financial institutions is a major roadblock in their efforts to survive this season. This is particularly concerning given that women own 12.3 million businesses[4] in the United States (making up 40% of all businesses), generate $1.8 trillion in sales, and employ over 9 million people each year.

Of the women-owned businesses, 5.4 million are majority-owned by women of color,[5] employ 2.1 million people, and generate $361 billion in annual revenues. In addition, in 2019, women opened 1,821 businesses every day[6] and of those new businesses, 64% were started by women of color.

Prior to the pandemic, it was well known that women, especially women of color, in addition to earning less on average than their white male counterparts, are less likely to get access to capital for their businesses. Women report facing both gender and racial biases when attempting to access capital, with bankers and investors asking questions more focused on their personal lives rather than about their businesses.

I can personally attest to this during my experience attempting to raise capital for Clever Girl Finance in 2018 and 2019. Through 90+ meetings with investors, I received comments by primarily white

[4]Maddie Shepherd, "Women-Owned Businesses: Statistics and Overview," Fundera, December 16, 2020, https://www.fundera.com/resources/women-owned-business-statistics
[5]"Women Business Owner Statistics," NAWBO, https://www.nawbo.org/resources/women-business-owner-statistics
[6]Shepherd, 2020.

male investors representing venture capital firms about how my children could be a hindrance to my ability to build a successful business, and why I should not tell investors I had children or that I was married because it indicated too much baggage as a founder.

I was also asked why I felt women of color did not have equal opportunities in America and questioned as to if it was truly a real issue or a gimmick to raise capital and whether it was proven that women of color cared about financial wellness, amongst many other sexist, gender-biased, and racially biased comments and questions. My efforts to raise capital at that time were unsuccessful.

My experiences, however, are not unique. Thousands of women in the Clever Girl Finance community have reported struggles with accessing capital to start, sustain, or grow their businesses. Thousands more female and minority founders continue to share their stories and struggles of being shut out of opportunities to get investment for their companies. In fact, women received only 2.2% of the $85 billion of venture capital invested in 2017; and of this capital raised by women, Latina women received 0.32% and black women received 0.0006%.[7] In 2018, the stat remained much the same with women again raising only 2.2% of the $130 billion of venture capital invested that year.[8]

With the pandemic severely impacting small businesses, the CARES Act funding for the emergency Paycheck Protection Program Loans

---

[7]Nina Zipkin, "Out of $85 Billion in VC Funding Last Year, Only 2.2 Percent Went to Female Founders. And Every Year, Women of Color Get Less Than 1 Percent of Total Funding," *Entrepreneur,* December 12, 2018, https://www.entrepreneur.com/article/324743
[8]Brock Blake, "Women Business Owners Still Face Difficulties in Obtaining Capital," *Forbes,* October 14, 2019, https://www.forbes.com/sites/brockblake/2019/10/14/women-business-capital/?sh=487b6617173e

has left many minority business owners shut out of the program despite millions of dollars in designated funds being set aside for minority and underserved borrowers. A report from the Center for Responsible Lending (CRL) dated April 6th, 2020, found that roughly 95% of Black-owned businesses and 91% of Latino-owned businesses "stand close to no chance of receiving a PPP loan through a mainstream bank or credit union."[9]

The main reasons for this shut out being that minority-owned businesses are less likely to have banking relationships and/or they lack access to financial education on how to access these funds. And banks are reluctant to make loans available to those they don't have relationships with or to those who have poor or no credit history even when they are able to show historical revenues and business potential.

To help counter this, Clever Girl Finance is helping women and women-owned businesses improve their finances, identify capital opportunities, and improve their chances of getting access to capital by supporting women with completely free content and online courses on business planning, including business financial planning and credit improvement amongst other resources.

We recognize financial education and improving financial wellness is key to closing the racial wealth gap and we are helping women, especially women of color, succeed with their personal finances and in starting and growing their businesses especially in these times of

---

[9]Center for Responsible Living, "The Paycheck Protection Program continues to be disadvantageous to smaller businesses, especially businesses owned by people of color and the self-employed," April 6, 2020, https://www.responsiblelending.org/sites/default/files/nodes/files/research-publication/crl-cares-act2-smallbusiness-apr2020.pdf?mod=article_inline

a pandemic where accessing capital is even more difficult and many women will have to find ways to generate capital on their own.

I strongly believe that government policy plays a critical role in improving the ability of women and minorities to gain access to much-needed capital right now. We desperately need policies in place that create benefits and funding opportunities for women and minority entrepreneurs. We need policies in place that encourage banking and other financial and venture capital institutions to prioritize and match capital to women and minority-owned businesses. Having these policies in place can have a major impact by enabling access to capital, fostering inclusion, and creating more transparency on the financial issues related to women and minority entrepreneurs.

There is no better time than now to seize the opportunity to effect change by putting policies in place focused on making capital more accessible to this currently underserved group.

Thank you for this opportunity, and I look forward to working with the committee in the future.

Sincerely,
Bola Sokunbi
Founder/CEO Clever Girl Finance

I shared my honest thoughts and experiences with the committee, which I believe is reflective of the experiences of many women and minorities everywhere. Having the experience to write this statement for the record was an incredible opportunity.

The year 2020 taught me a greater form of resilience. It reminded me that life is fragile and can change unexpectedly and in a devastating and painful way. But as human beings, we are capable of overcoming challenges, despite how difficult they might be. 2020 challenged me to step further outside of my comfort zone and further into my purpose for the greater good of helping other people with my talents, my resources, and my voice. It was a reminder (not that I ever forget) of who I am as a black woman in America and a reminder of the fact that I must continue to instill values and confidence in my children. The experience of 2020 was also an important reminder to prioritize what's most important to me in life. It's being present with my family and friends. It's my mental wellness. It's being able to give back and use my dollars intentionally to support women-owned and minority-owned businesses whenever I can. It's doing the important work that we do at Clever Girl Finance and making sure that what we're doing continues to have a direct and positive impact on the women who join our community wanting to achieve financial wellness.

WHAT I'VE LEARNED

If there's anything I took away from 2020, it was a firm reminder that life is short and I need to hold the people I love close and tell them what they mean to me every chance I get. I was reminded of our resilience as human beings and focused on being a better person. I learned that pursuing my mission of making a positive impact in the world through my business, no matter how small, is more important and more rewarding than any short-term profits. Most importantly I was reminded never to take anything I have for granted. My mantra is, "Gratitude, always."

LET'S TALK ABOUT YOU

As you read this, I challenge you to prioritize what's most important to you in your life. Life is short, and it's unpredictable. But you can decide the actions you want to take to pursue your goals, your passions, your purpose, and your prosperity, despite what life may throw at you in the short term.

2020 was painful, but life is worth living and more so authentically and on your own terms. Here are some questions to help you reflect:

- What was most challenging in your life during 2020?
- How did you get through the year?
- What positive experiences did you have in 2020?
- In what ways did you grow and evolve as a person?
- Based on your experience in 2020, how are you choosing to live your life differently and purposefully, knowing how short life is?

Take what you learned about your experience going through 2020 (or a recent difficult year) and use it to map out how you intend to be more intentional with the way you live your life going forward.

CHAPTER 10

Proudly Black, Female, and Successful

You work hard.
Acknowledge
yourself and
celebrate your
successes.

The path of my life has led me to this place, right here, where I can describe myself as proudly black, female, and successful. All of my experiences, whether good or bad, have made me the woman I am today. Over the years, I've built up my confidence, defined who I am as a woman, gotten clear on my purpose, and chosen to prosper. . .on my own terms— and it's been quite the journey.

Does it sound arrogant of me to describe myself as proudly black, female, and successful? In my opinion, no. Not at all. I've worked my butt off to get here. It's been hard work, sweat, and tears, so I'm giving myself my own roses, and I encourage you to do the same. You deserve all the bouquets, and you don't need to wait for anyone to hand them to you.

There was, however, a time when I thought talking about success and achievements was equivalent to being arrogant and bragging. In fact, when I first started Clever Girl Finance, I described myself as self-employed, and that was it. When it came time to update the LinkedIn profile I set up for myself as a business owner, I was not entirely comfortable using the words *CEO* or *founder*. Looking back, I think it was part imposter syndrome and part feeling like those titles were reserved for other people, not women like me.

Yes, sometimes talking about success and achievements— depending on the motivations of the person speaking and how they come across—can seem arrogant. But in the context of this book and me talking about my success, my motivations are to set the stage so other women can win and surpass the success I have achieved.

As I've gotten older, with a daughter of my own and a continuously growing Clever Girl Finance audience base, I've realized that talking about success and achievements—especially as a black woman and woman of color, a demographic that has been boxed into all kinds of negative stereotypes that don't often include success, wealth, or prosperity—is not only empowering to other women, but it is also motivational. And I love to see it when women are not only celebrated but when they also celebrate themselves.

Seeing a woman celebrate herself is a signal to young girls and other women that it's perfectly normal to be confident and successful. It makes success and the pursuit of big dreams and goals attainable for the women who hear your story. This is what my mom wanted me to see when she chose to change her life trajectory by going to college with me in tow in her mid-thirties, and this is what I want my daughter to see—successful women. Confidence and success as a woman are not shameful or something to be shy about, regardless of what anyone might want you to believe. Whether you are married, single, divorced, a mother, have chosen not to get married or not to have kids—whatever. You can be successful, period. There are no status criteria to be successful in your own right and on your own terms.

In the years since I started Clever Girl Finance, I've gained confidence in sharing my title as "CEO and female founder" because I want my daughter to know there's nothing she can't do. I've built and continue to build a business of value that not only empowers other women but also positively impacts their lives. And in all of this, my day-to-day responsibilities as a woman running a business (including being a leader to my team, setting the vision for my company, and executing growth strategies), is very much akin to any other CEO's experience, regardless of their gender or how much larger or more successful their business is than mine.

But more importantly, since staring Clever Girl Finance, I've recognized that representation matters. Women need to see other women who look like them in the places they aspire to be, accomplishing the goals they want to achieve, and chasing the dreams they want to chase. I imagine that if my mom and the other incredible women in my life had never motivated me to succeed or to be proud of who I was or to celebrate my accomplishments, I would not be here. Clever Girl Finance would not exist, and you would not be reading this book. Perhaps I would be somewhere thinking less of myself, doubting my ability to succeed, and conforming to whatever standards are placed on me as a woman.

Imagine if there were no other women for us to be inspired by because they never shared their stories. How many of us would feel bold enough to step out and pursue our own dreams? Sure, some of us would make attempts at our dreams, but a lot of us wouldn't, simply because we're hardwired to aspire to what we can see, what we can relate to, or what has been attained before us. This is why celebrating your success is so important.

One thing I do, however, want to be clear about when it comes to my success and the accomplishments that I share is that I did not do this alone. I am not superhuman with superpowers. I am a regular human. I get tired. I feel vulnerable. I make tons of mistakes. My emotions run the full gamut, and I cry (a lot). People will sometimes describe me as "self-made." But the truth is, I've never been comfortable with that term. I personally don't refer to myself that way even when others do, and the reason is simple. I am not self-made. Yes, I've put in the work. But a lot of people have contributed to the makings of who I am and what I've been able to accomplish, so I cannot in full sincerity stand up and say, *"Hi, my name is Bola, and I made it all by myself."* It's just not true.

There are so many women in my family, including my mom, who set the stage for me. There are my mentors and advisors and every woman who's pulled me aside to bare her soul, give me advice, and share her lessons. There are my friends and family, including my husband, who constantly motivate and root for me. There is the team behind everything you see at Clever Girl Finance. And there's also our community who has shared their successes and how we have helped them on their journey to financial wellness—which in turn inspires me to keep going and to do more and to be better. All of these incredibly amazing people, in one way or an other, have contributed to who I am today.

I will be the first to tell you, I am privileged: Privileged to be alive as we navigate the aftermath of an insane pandemic. Privileged to have been born to parents who supported, encouraged, and sacrificed for me as a young child because they wanted me to have opportunities. Privileged to have had the opportunity to attend good schools and to have had an international experience. Privileged to live in America, a land of opportunity compared to many other places in the world, despite its own challenges and shortcomings. Privileged to be who I am and to come from where I come from.

Privilege is not a bad thing, and the fact that you are reading this book means you, too, can list out your own privileges. However, the truth is that when it comes to privilege, not everyone takes advantage of the opportunities it gives them. I've never wanted that to be me, especially knowing my family background. My goal is to leverage every opportunity my privilege gives me to do good, open doors, and create impact. This means ignoring the naysayers and the doubters and the people who refuse to acknowledge all the hard work I've put in to get here, including the people who flat out just don't want to see me to succeed. I can't let them get in the way of my progress or block my blessings. It means having people around me to keep me accountable and to hold me to what I say I'm going to do. It means not getting comfortable in my comfort zone, getting out of my own way, and pushing myself to keep going because there's still so much I have to do to further my mission and my purpose. It means intentionally choosing to prosper for the women who came before me and for my children and my children's children who will come after me. So, when I call myself proudly black, female, and successful, I'm not saying it because it sounds cool. I'm saying it because of what it truly means to me.

WHAT I'VE LEARNED

I am very much still on a journey of personal and entrepreneurial growth, but I've learned that sharing my experiences, including my failures and my wins, is empowering to other women as they go on their own journeys. It also gives me an opportunity to reflect on how far I've come. I've learned to be proud of my accomplishments and that it's okay for me to acknowledge and celebrate myself because I know how hard I've worked to get here.

LET'S TALK ABOUT YOU

As you journey through your life, it's important to recognize your personal accomplishments and applaud yourself for them. (It can be the ultimate confidence boost!) Here are some questions to help you reflect:

- Do you acknowledge and celebrate your successes? If so, how do you do it?
- What makes you most proud when you reflect on the different areas in your life today?
- How can you do a better job of acknowledging yourself more often?
- List out 10 accomplishments or successes you're most proud of (no matter how small!). Refer back to this list when you need motivation.

Start keeping track of your accomplishments and remind yourself why you are deserving; you've worked hard. And remember, no wins are too small to celebrate. Progress is progress is progress.

What's Next?

You've chosen to prosper, and now it's time to take action.

This is my story and my journey so far. And while it might be vastly different from yours, my hope is that you walk away from this book inspired to go out and pursue your own goals and dreams harder than before and on your own terms. If you've been reflecting on the various questions I asked throughout this book, this is a great time to go over the answers you wrote down and lay out the action steps you want to take for your own career, business, relationships, finances and life moving forward. You are here, and you've chosen to prosper and now it's time to take action.

Choosing to prosper is a choice I intentionally made for myself. I think about the people who have set the stage and allowed me to be where I am today. I constantly remind myself that my grandmothers wanting better for their children took action to create that better life, despite adversity and despite taboo. They chose to prosper as best as they could. I am grateful, and I recognize that the baton has been passed on to me and it's my job to continue to take my own actions and to continue to be intentional with setting the stage for my own children, so they, too, can have a better life and live their own lives on their own terms.

Being intentional about choosing to prosper is you deciding to do well, regardless of the odds stacked against you. It's about choosing to live the best life you can, regardless of where you come from. If you are here, you've chosen to prosper, too. And the great part about choosing to prosper is that you have everything it takes to make this decision and to go after your prosperity regardless of the adversity or roadblocks you might face. The truth is, there will always be adversity, and there will always be roadblocks. But how you choose to deal with them and navigate around them can make all the difference.

You are in a unique position to make a difference in your personal life, for your family and your broader community. This is my story, but it continues. I still have a long way to go—and so much more to accomplish with Clever Girl Finance and in my life overall. So, I continue on with being the best mother and wife that I can be, with using my voice to take a stand to advocate for other women, and with building a business that will have massive positive impact. What next steps will you take starting right now as you choose to prosper?

Index